This book is absolutely riveting and speaks to where the church is in this dispensation, and will definitely transcend through generations to come.

—Pastor Timothy Washington
St. Mary's M.B. Church
Chicago, IL

This book is a best seller! It will encourage you not to accept a defeated lifestyle and to live victoriously.

—Pastor Sadie L. Henderson
Temple of Deliverance Ministries
Waco, TX

THE
STRUGGLE
IS OVER

THE
STRUGGLE
IS OVER
THE KINGDOM OF HEAVEN HAS COME!

GAIL L. THOMAS

TATE PUBLISHING & *Enterprises*

Published by Tate Publishing & Enterprises, LLC
127 E. Trade Center Terrace | Mustang, Oklahoma 73064 USA
1.888.361.9473 | www.tatepublishing.com

Tate Publishing is committed to excellence in the publishing industry. The company reflects the philosophy established by the founders, based on Psalm 68:11,
"The Lord gave the word and great was the company of those who published it."

Book design copyright © 2009 by Tate Publishing, LLC. All rights reserved.
Cover design by Tyler Evans
Interior design by Jeff Fisher

Published in the United States of America
ISBN: 978-1-61566-100-8
1. Religion, Christian Life, Devotional
2. Religion, Christian Life, Inspirational
09.10.27

DEDICATION

To the many men and women of God that believe that the kingdom of heaven is presently reigning, and therefore, desires not to miss the move of God. I say unto you: March on soldiers; rule and reign until he comes.

To sisterhood and all its splendor and glory. Behold how good and how pleasant it is for us to dwell together in unity! May we continue to run and tell the story just like Mary did on that resurrection morning.

To God the Father, God the Son, and God the Holy Ghost, I thank you, for you are always right. *The struggle is over because the kingdom of heaven has come.* Truly, there is nothing impossible to them that believe.

FOREWORD

Minister Gail Thomas is an anointed powerhouse working for God. She has a deep concern for the body of Christ to learn how to live within the kingdom's principles; thereby, causing manifestations on earth as they are in heaven. Over our 30 years of fellowship, I have consistently watched her execute God's word, not only in the spiritual realm but also in the natural realm. I strongly believe that reading *The Struggle is Over: The Kingdom of Heaven Has Come* and applying its principles and spiritual wisdom to your life, will allow you to see strongholds and bondages destroyed.

This book will help you identify specific areas of your life that do not line up with the principles of kingdom living. As you take heed to the spiritual keys of this book, it will cause you to die to the deeds of the flesh, walk in God's supernatural power, and therefore take over the Father's business.

In II Chronicles 20:15, the Word of God tells us that the battle is not ours; it's the Lord's. This book teaches that we should not struggle but continue in the good fight of faith as the power of God worketh within us.

—Co-Pastor Annie Moore
Friendship Pentecostal Church
Lawton, Oklahoma

TABLE OF CONTENTS

INTRODUCTION

When I consider the struggle that many face and have faced because of lack of faith and/or lack of knowledge in the Word of God, it saddens me. Everything that we need for success was given to us from the foundation of the world. God himself said that we were created in his image and likeness. Therefore, the seed of God abides in us. God himself caused us to exist and brought us into being. He has given us the ability to succeed in every area of our lives. God's Word declares that he sent Jesus that we would have life and that more abundantly. As God's children, we have lived beneath our rights and privileges long enough. It is not nor will it ever be the will of Father God for his children to struggle.

Some would choose to believe that the struggle would be over if they had all the money that they needed. On the other hand, many don't believe that the children of God should be financially prosperous. Therefore, they struggle daily to meet their basic needs. *The Struggle Is Over Because the Kingdom of Heaven Has Come* is more than about being a pauper or being financially stable. It is about knowing the will of God for our lives, as well as walking in the authority and power that has been given to us through the complete work of Jesus Christ. Whereby, we can see the expressed will of God being manifested here on earth. Manifestation of heaven on earth will only be expedited when we start to work the Word of God, for it truly works. In order for us to see the struggle reversed, we must abide by God's written instructions, submit to the ministry of the Holy Spirit and follow the leadership of the five-fold ministry, which consists of apostles, prophets, evangelist, pastors, and teachers. This submission along with patience will help us to stay focused on the Father's will for our lives and reveal to us those things that have prevented us from having dominion; as well as, instruct us on how to defeat a life of struggle.

God continues to let it be known that we are his ambassadors: spiritual representatives of the kingdom of God here on earth, who have been appointed with the highest rank possible for doing kingdom business. If we were to consider natural ambassadors or diplomatic officials from other countries, we would see that they have the best that their country can afford them when they are representing abroad. That country would never allow us to see their dignitaries struggle because it is a representation of them. Why then would Almighty God, the One who declares that the earth is his and the fullness thereof, the world and all that dwell therein, allow us to struggle when we are a representation of the kingdom of heaven? It would be like God is unable to care for his own after allowing us to be birthed into the earth, and we all know better than that.

God had a plan from the beginning of time that we would commune with him and show forth his glory. Today that plan still remains in place. The great thing about God's plan is that it never had anything to do with us struggling. So let us stop struggling and start reigning. For his kingdom has come, now it is time that his will be done on earth just as it is in heaven.

Chapter 1

THE STRUGGLE

What Caused the Struggle?

When I pondered the word *struggle,* many thoughts started to flow through my mind. Immediately, I visualized pulling and tugging between the spirit and natural world, or between good and evil, as though there were a tug-of-war going on. Yes, some type of contest, where two forces are pulling in opposition of each other to become the dominant power or influence by reason of defeat.

According to the book of Genesis in the Bible, a tug-of-war between good and evil went on between Adam, Eve, and the serpent, until the serpent finally defeated the man whom God had created in his image and in his likeness to rule and have dominion on earth.

The Bible goes on to say,

And the Lord God formed man of the dust of the ground, and breathed into his nostrils the breath of life; and man became a living soul. And the Lord God planted a garden eastward in Eden; and there he put the man whom he had formed. And out of the ground made the Lord God to grow every tree that is pleasant to the sight, and good for food; the tree of life also in the midst of the garden, and the tree of knowledge of good and evil.... And the Lord God took the man, and put him into the garden of Eden to dress it and to keep it. And the Lord God commanded the man, saying, Of every tree of the garden thou mayest freely eat: But of the tree of the knowledge of good and evil, thou shalt not eat of it: for in the day that thou eatest thereof thou shalt surely die. And the Lord God said, It is not good that the man should be alone; I will make him an help meet for him ... Now the serpent was more subtil than any beast of the field which the Lord God had made. And he said unto the woman, Yea, hath God said, Ye shall not eat of every tree of the garden? And the woman said unto the serpent, We may eat of the fruit of the trees of the garden: But of the fruit of the tree which is in the midst of the garden, God hath said, Ye shall not eat of it, neither shall ye touch it, lest ye die. And the serpent said unto the woman, Ye shall not surely die: For God doth know that in the day ye eat thereof, then your eyes shall be opened, and ye shall be as gods, knowing good and evil. And when the woman saw that the tree was good for food, and that it was pleasant to the eyes, and a tree to be desired to make one wise, she took of the fruit thereof, and did eat, and gave also unto her

husband with her; and he did eat. And the eyes of
them both were opened …

Gen. 2:7–9, 15–18, 3:1–7

The Word of God clearly shows us from the
beginning of time that the enemy has strove with
the children of God in an attempt to give us a false
representation of our Father's love and to keep us
from the best that the Father has for us. The pull
of deception and underhandedness that the enemy
used on Adam and Eve, God's freewill beings,
enticed them to disobey God. This caused betrayal
of trust and confidence in their Father and what
he had planned, prepared, and provided for them.

As Adam took his first bite of the fruit from
the tree of the knowledge of good and evil, man
became responsible for his own well-being, success, and prosperity because of his disobedience.
This was not the will of the Father then, nor is it
the will of the Father now. Adam's disobedience to
and rejection of the Father set something detest-
able into motion for all mankind and the conse-
quences immediately followed.

And unto Adam he said, Because thou hast hear-
kened unto the voice of thy wife, and hast eaten
of the tree, of which I commanded thee, saying,
Thou shalt not eat of it: cursed is the ground for
thy sake; in sorrow shalt thou eat of it all the days
of thy life; Thorns also and thistles shall it bring
forth to thee; and thou shalt eat the herb of the
field; In the sweat of thy face shalt thou eat bread,
till thou return unto the ground; for out of it wast
thou taken: for dust thou art, and unto dust shalt

thou return ... And the Lord God said, Behold, the man is become as one of us, to know good and evil; and now, lest he put forth his hand, and take also of the tree of life, and eat, and live forever: Therefore the Lord God sent him forth from the garden of Eden, to till the ground from whence he was taken.

Genesis 3:17–19, 22–23

God's declaration to Adam signified that he had no choice but to postpone his plans for his son to walk in dominion. Even though the Father knew that he had ordained Adam to walk in dominion, he had no legal choice but to allow Adam to pursue after the course that he had chosen. Like Adam and Eve, we too have valiantly and foolishly refused to follow our Father's instructions or to be led and taught by the Holy Spirit. Some of us continue to eat the forbidden fruit of self-reliance and disobedience that the enemy is dangling in our faces. His goal is to prevent us from walking in our rightful place of dominion and authority, where we were empowered to rule and reign. Therefore, the spirit of independence, self-sufficiency, and self-rule has become man's governing force. Thus catapulting all men headfirst into what I call "The Struggle."

Over our lifespan, we have become so closely intertwined and intimate with the spirit of independence that we have allowed it to become our God. The spirit of self-rule and self-will has brought many of us to a place of desperation, despondency, and destruction that we no longer know our purpose or destiny, and this is exactly what the enemy yearns for.

The Rescue Plan

Thanks be to God. There is good news for us. Our Father had a plan to rescue us from the beginning of time.

Immediately after the fall of man,

> And the Lord God said unto the woman, What is this that thou hast done? And the woman said, The serpent beguiled me, and I did eat. And the Lord God said unto the serpent, Because thou hast done this, thou art cursed above all cattle, and above every beast of the field; upon thy belly shalt thou go, and dust shalt thou eat all the days of thy life: And I will put enmity between thee and the woman, and between thy seed and her seed; it shall bruise thy head, and thou shalt bruise his heel.
>
> Gen. 3:13–15

These scriptures are our open door back into the dominion and authority that we lost so long ago. God loved us so much that at the beginning of time he decreed that he would send his son Jesus to legally return to us what was lost during man's fall from dominion. Through many years of suffering, sorrow, and travail, God sent his only begotten son Jesus to defeat the devil by shedding his blood and dying for us. The Father then resurrected him from the dead and sat him on his right side of power, to rule and reign with him forever. This great act of love that Jesus showed toward us completed everything that needed to be accomplished to empower us to walk back into dominion.

Another great thing about these scriptures is that they allow us to see that there will always be hatred and hostility between the devil and God's children. Knowing this we must protect our off-spring, ancestry, legacy, and generations to come by giving our whole heart to Father-God, our Lord and Savior, Jesus Christ. We must as well teach our children the significance of being a Godly seed. By doing this we will instill in them the importance of loving the Lord with all their heart, mind, soul and strength and therefore; bringing forth a generation of upright children.

Psalms 112:1–2 says,

> "Praise ye the Lord. Blessed is the man that feareth the Lord, that delighteth greatly in his command-ments. His seed shall be mighty upon earth: the generation of the upright shall be blessed."

It is true that Jesus defeated the devil on our behalf. However, it is now up to us to keep him under our feet. Just as God spoke victory to the woman and defeat to the serpent, we must speak victory to our seed from the time of conception and let them know that they were predestined before the foundation of the world to do great and marvelous exploits for their God and King. We must tell them about the power of the seed; it has the power inside of it to produce after its kind and that they are God's seed. They must know that they are *Generation Upright:* A holy seed, a righ-teous seed, a holy nation, a royal priesthood, and a chosen generation which has been set aside for our King's service.

Satan knows the importance of a Godly seed and with every opportunity given, he tries to destroy it. For ages he has tried to blind us and prevent us from recognizing the power of our Godly seed. It's amazing to me that many times the world realizes just how important our seed is yet, we don't. If we would just take a look back during biblical times and see what happened to God's seed when the Israelites were conquered by another country and king, we would see that the king always wanted the best seed. He would take the finest seed; those that were full of wisdom, knowledge, and that understood the sciences so that they could stand before him in his palace. Those like the Daniel's, the Hananiah's, the Mishael's, and the Azariah's; then he would immediately try to separate them from who they were and what they believed by giving them other names such as Belteshazzar, Shadrach, Meshach, and Abednego.

Today there is no difference. The world, which is ruled by the devil, still wants our children. Therefore, we must teach them their importance and purpose. We must let our children know how important they are to God and to us. "And God said, Let the earth bring forth grass, the herb yielding seed, and the fruit tree yielding fruit after his kind, whose seed is in itself, upon the earth: and it was so." (Genesis 1:11) Look at this; every seed knows what its purpose is. The apple seed knows that its purpose is to produce apples; and the orange seed will only produce oranges. However, many times our seed doesn't know what its purpose is. Since we have been created in God's image, we are obligated by the God in us to talk to the God in them; so that our seed also will produce fruit after its kind. Fruit to be used by our Lord. We no longer can appeal to our children's flesh; we must start to minister and speak to the God in them.

This is what God said about Abraham concerning his children,

> "Seeing that Abraham shall surely become a great and mighty nation, and all the nations of the earth shall be blessed in him? For I know him, that he will command his children and his household after him, and they shall keep the way of the Lord, to do justice and judgment; that the Lord may bring upon Abraham that which he hath spoken of him."
>
> Genesis 18:18–19

God planned that we would be a part of a great and mighty nation. As we continue to walk by faith like Abraham, the father of faith, we must also do as Abraham and command our children to walk in the things of God. I believe that this can only be accomplished by speaking to the God in them. God knows the power of the seed; that it has the ability to produce blessings or curses. God's purpose, our heritage, culture and legacy are in our seed. This is why our seed must know that they have been called with a holy calling. They have been chosen to be a generation of the upright, and surely they are!

I can hear some of you thinking about your

seed that have chosen to live their lives outside of the will of God. They have told you that there is a "generation gap" or that there is a vast difference in your values and life styles. Don't believe the lie; they are just trying to determine what kind of seed they are and whose seed they are. You know deep down in their hearts they know what kind of seed they are. Be assured that God doesn't have any mutated seeds just disobedient seeds. Be encouraged and know that he still has our children, his seeds in the palms of his hands. No matter where our children are during this time of their lives, or what we may see with our natural eyes we must choose to speak the Word of God over their lives. We must believe God to give our seed the victory over the struggles in their lives just as he is doing in ours. Isn't that why God sent his only begotten Son, Jesus (his only seed) into the world?

Now it is up to us to make the right choices and adjustments to rule and reign as heirs of the promise just as we have been created to.

Our time is far spent. No longer can our focus be on the petty things of this world. There must be a renewing, a transformation in the way that we have been thinking and operating. The kingdom of heaven is greater than what you or I ever imagined. As we look at one facet of the kingdom, we can clearly see the importance of generational reigning.

Since we have been enlightened by the Spirit of God on why it is so important for us to walk in dominion, we have no choice but to rise to the occasion. If by any chance we choose not to, the blood of generations to come will be upon our hands. The

Father has equipped us, as well as our seed, with all that we need to succeed. He has placed himself in us in the person of the Holy Spirit to lead and guide us.

Thousands of years later, the same tug-a-war continues to exist between the devil and God's children, the fight of good verses evil, the fight to separate us from our Father's love. Surely, we should be able to see clearer than those that have come before us. If we can see with more clarity, then no longer should we be lured away by the cunning devices of the enemy. Our opponent's trickery has not changed. We must continue to resist the spirit of independence, self-sufficiency and self-rule and send it back to hell from where it came.

God's words have not changed. If God told us to subdue the earth and have dominion over it, that is what he expects. Yes! The struggle is over because the kingdom of heaven has come, and we have entry into it through our Lord and Savior, Jesus Christ. The open door into the kingdom of heaven stands in front of you. What are you waiting for?

Jesus continues to say,

> Behold, I stand at the door, and knock: if any man hear my voice, and open the door, I will come in to him, and will sup with him, and he with me. To him that overcometh will I grant to sit with me in my throne, even as I also overcame, and am set down with my Father in his throne. He that hath an ear, let him hear what the Spirit saith unto the churches.
>
> Revelation 3:20–22

Chapter 2

IT'S NO TIME TO STRUGGLE, IT'S TIME TO FIGHT!

The Day My Struggle Turned into My Fight

I had come to the conclusion that I didn't want to struggle any longer. However, I didn't know where I would go from there. It seemed as though thousands of questions started to bombard my mind, and the words of my heart went something like this: Am I in your will? Am I doing what you want me to do? *I need answers!*

I am tired of going around the same mountain of not enough, not knowing what your will is for me. I'm tired of hitting and missing, trying to make things happen on my own. To be honest, I'm tired of acting as though there is no struggle and that I'm okay. I'm not okay! God, your Word said to work out my salvation with fear and trembling. Lord, you know that I have been trying to work out my salvation through obeying your Word. I know that you are not a liar and that your Word is true. So what is the problem? Am I in a holding pattern? Am I being tried? All I know is that I need answers and you are the only One that can give them to me.

Father, I'm not trying to live a life without difficulties. I know that your Word says that we would have tribulations in this world. Knowing your direction and intentions for me will help me endure whatever I need to go through. I don't want to have a form of godliness and deny your power. You truly are my Father, God, Lord, Savior, and King, and I desire to do things your way. So Father, I'm in your hands; help me to get out of the struggle. Help me not be like an ostrich with his head in the sand. Help me to be true to myself. I don't want to be blind. I don't want to have an independent spirit. I know that I can't make anything happen without you. Then I heard the Spirit of God say, *"Struggle will I not, but I am willing to fight!"*

That quick the Spirit of God spoke to me. More clarity came as I pondered on this revelation that I had just received. He was making it clear that I am in a fight: not only physically but spiritually, mentally, emotionally, relationally, and financially. *The Holy Spirit made it so clear that if I was willing to fight, he would fight for me and with me.* He was willing to help me subdue and defeat the enemy of my soul and to stop the struggle. When the Spirit of God spoke those words to me, it was as though a light came on; new insight was downloaded into my spiritual being.

There had to be a transformation; an exchange from my old way of thinking. Instead of thinking that I was going to war to win a fight, I now had to take the position and believe that I had won the fight before I ever entered it. I had known for years that I was in a fight. When I started to reminisce about my childhood, I remembered that I didn't like to fight, nor did I want to, but if I had to, I would. That same physical mindset now had to be transitioned into the spiritual realm. Today, as a child of God I still don't like to fight, but I have learned that I have no choice and neither do you. The difference now is knowing that when we go into battle, we already have the victory.

Pressing into the Kingdom and Taking It by Force!

The fall of Adam caused many problems that mankind still contends with. Fighting for what God has purposed for us from creation is one of them. We have been chosen to be victorious and to be triumphant; but to attain this, we must therefore, fight!When I thought about the fight to obtain what God has for us, the words that Jesus spoke came to mind: "And from the days of John the Baptist until now the kingdom of heaven suffereth violence, and the violent take it by force" (St. Matthew 11:12). The New International Version (NIV) says, "And from the days of John the Baptist until now the kingdom of heaven has been forcibly advancing and the forceful men lay hold of it" (Matthew 11:12).

[1] Many times people have asked me, " What is the kingdom of heaven?" They have read or heard this scripture, and it stirs up excitement in them. It gives them a desire to seek after the kingdom of heaven; however, they are not sure what it is or how to take it by force. I could understand exactly how they were feeling. As long as I can remember, Christians have had a lack of understanding about the kingdom of heaven. I can recall in Sunday school when we would discuss scriptures about the kingdom of heaven. I was never able to get an answer that set well with my heart or spirit. It was as though most believed that the kingdom of heaven had *not* come and that we would receive the kingdom of heaven (whatever that meant) when we arrived over in glory. As a result of not having an understanding of the kingdom of heaven, I believe that this has contributed to our struggle.

One reason that there has probably been so much confusion about the kingdom of heaven is because Jesus did not leave us with a concise definition of what the "kingdom of heaven" meant (*Baker* 451). Therefore, we must work with what God has revealed to us through his written Word and Holy Spirit. With the information that we have about the kingdom of heaven, we know that the kingdom of heaven is the rule, reign, and authority of God. It is the literal governing of God in heaven and in the earth realm, where God has sovereign power and is able to get the results that he desires. God's kingdom, the kingdom of heaven, is being manifested daily in the natural and supernatural by the seen and unseen work of God in the hearts, affairs, and lives of men.

I believe that the Apostle Paul's Damascus road experience is a great example of the rule of God in heaven and in earth. The scripture says,

> And Saul, yet breathing out threatenings and slaughter against the disciples of the Lord, went unto the high priest, And desired of him letters to Damascus to the synagogues, that if he found any of this way, whether they were men or women, he might bring them bound unto Jerusalem. And as he journeyed, he came near Damascus: and suddenly there shined round about him a light from heaven: And he fell to the earth, and heard a voice saying unto him, Saul, Saul, why persecutest thou me? And he said, Who are thou, Lord? And the Lord said, I am Jesus whom thou persecutest: it is hard for thee to kick against the pricks. And he trembling and astonished said, Lord, what wilt thou have me to do? And the Lord said unto him, Arise, and go into the city, and it shall be told thee what thou must do. And the men, which journeyed with him stood speechless, hearing a voice, but seeing no man. And Saul arose from the earth; and when his eyes were opened, he saw no man: but they led him by the hand, and brought him into Damascus. And he was three days without sight, and neither did eat nor drink. And there was a certain disciple at Damascus, named Ananias; and to him said the Lord in a vision, Ananias. And he said, Behold, I am here, Lord. And the Lord said unto him, Arise, and go into the street which is called Straight, and

enquire in the house of Judas for one called Saul, of Tarsus for, behold, he prayeth, And hath seen in a vision a man named Ananias coming in, and putting his hand on him, that he might receive his sight. Then Ananias answered, Lord, I have heard by many of this man, how much evil he hath done to thy saints at Jerusalem: And here he hath authority from the chief priests to bind all that call on thy name. But the Lord said unto him, go thy way: for he is a chosen vessel unto me, to bear my name before the Gentiles, and kings, and the children of Israel: For I will show how great things he must suffer for my name's sake. And Ananias went his way, and entered into the house; and putting his hands on him said, Brother Saul, the Lord, even Jesus, that appeared unto thee in the way as thou camest, hath sent me, that thou mightest receive thy sight, and the be filled with the Holy Ghost. And immediately there fell from his eyes as it had been scales: and he received sight forthwith, and arose, and was baptized … Then had the churches rest throughout all Judea and Galilee and Samaria, and were edified; and walking in the fear of the Lord, and in the comfort of the Holy Ghost, were multiplied.

Acts 9:1–18, 31

God in his omnipotence allowed his Son to reach down from heaven and cause his will to be fulfilled in the earth; thereby, showing that all things are instruments in the hands of God and that he has the ability to transform the lives of men and women for his glory.

This glimpse of Paul's life showed us more than the kingdom of heaven being manifested in the earth. It showed us that Paul had an earnest desire for the things of God. However, because of his ignorance of who Jesus was and what Jesus' death and resurrection had accomplished, it becomes an instrument in the hands of the devil. Paul eagerly persecuted the people of God and put them to death, believing that he was doing the work of God. He showed us how we can cause the kingdom of heaven to suffer violence or hostility when we do not have an understanding of the ways of God and when we attempt to do God's work in our own strength and understanding.

Things, however, changed that day when God's son, Jesus, spoke from heaven to earth and declared to Paul that he was in error and to stop persecuting the body of Christ. Almost instantaneously God's divine will for Paul's life came to fruition. Paul's acceptance of Jesus Christ and answer to the heavenly call caused him to stop the enemy's assault against the kingdom of heaven and become the violent. We too can become violent and stop the enemy's assault against the kingdom of heaven when we are obedient to the will of God. This allows us to take back what is rightfully ours. Paul is recorded in history as being responsible for bringing the gospel to the Gentiles. He also is one of the largest contributors of the Bible. There is no doubt that the end of Paul's life was greater than his beginning as he forcefully advanced the kingdom of heaven by the Spirit of the living God.

The Kingdom Is at Hand!

I have always taken God's Word to mean just what it says. For me, if Jesus said that the kingdom of heaven was at hand, then it was at hand; plain and simple. There is one thing that I know without a doubt in my heart (if I don't know anything else) that the kingdom of heaven has indeed come. [2]I believe right now that the kingdom of heaven is actively advancing so that the will of God will be fulfilled on the earth through us. The Bible clearly states in Matthew 3:1–2, "In those days came John the Baptist, preaching in the wilderness of Judaea, and saying, Repent ye: for the kingdom of heaven is at hand." Just as John is nearing the end of his God-ordained purpose, Jesus steps into his public ministry declaring the very same words that John had proclaimed earlier, " … Repent: for the kingdom of heaven is at hand" (Matthew 4:17).

How powerful and exhilarating it must have been for John the Baptist, the forerunner of Jesus, to know that he was helping to usher in the kingdom of heaven. The words "at hand" simply mean "now." "Now" means at this point in the series of events that things will no longer be the same. It is also used to introduce a new command, reproof, or request. Jesus, knowing that he had come to fulfill all righteousness and establish God's kingdom here on earth, therefore, introduces a new command. This command was for us to immediately change the way we were doing business. No longer would it be business as usual. No longer would we bind up and forbid things like the Pharisees and Sadducees, the religious leaders of Jesus time; we would now set free, deliver, and give liberty to the captives just as Jesus had.

Jesus, knowing the hearts of all men and knowing how faithless we can be, gives us another witness that would be irrefutable regarding the kingdom of heaven being at hand even 2,000 years later. Matthew 12:22–29 says,

> Then was brought unto him one possessed with a devil, blind, and dumb: and he healed him, insomuch that the blind and dumb both spake and saw. And all the people were amazed, and said, Is not this the son of David? But when the Pharisees heard it, they said, this fellow doth not cast out devils, but by Beelzebub the prince of the devils. And Jesus knew their thoughts, and said unto them, Every kingdom divided against itself is brought to desolation; and every city or house divided against itself shall not stand: And if Satan cast out Satan, he is divided against himself; how shall then his kingdom stand? And if Beelzebub cast out devils, by whom do your children cast them out? Therefore they shall be your judges. *But if I cast out devils by the Spirit of God, then the kingdom of God is come unto you.* Or else how can one enter into a strong man's house, and spoil his goods, except he first bind the strong man? And then he will spoil his house.

If the Pharisees would have just given God the praise and glory that was due him, this confrontation could have been avoided. The Pharisees or anyone else that has ever witnessed or experienced the intrusive and degrading offense of demon possession or the casting out of demons know that the Spirit of God can only bring this unruliness under submission and defeat. It is just like the devil to try to prevent God from getting the glory and honor that is due him. Therefore, Jesus takes control of the situation and assures that God gets his glory while giving the Pharisees something to think about. He allows the Pharisees to be their own judge about how their children were casting out devils; if they thought that he was casting them out by the prince of the devil.

Jesus then set the record straight and let the religious leaders know that it was not by power or the will of man that the spirit of darkness was bound up, because this type of supernatural deliverance could only happen by the Spirit of God and that God's kingdom was being fulfilled before their very eyes. Jesus knew that the only way that any kingdom could be defeated was by a greater kingdom defeating it. Jesus makes it very plain that he is the greater kingdom.

Since there is no doubt that God's kingdom is presently ruling and reigning, we must submit to his authority, divine will, and ways. Willingly and obediently following God's leadership will allow us to advance the kingdom of heaven because we are being lead by no one other than God himself. When faced with the question from the Pharisees: When shall the kingdom of God come?; Jesus answered, "The kingdom of God cometh not with observation: Neither shall they say, Lo here! or, lo there!

For, behold, the kingdom of God is within you." Luke 17:20–21

Knowing that the kingdom of heaven abides within us, we can declare: The struggle is over because the kingdom of heaven has come!

Don't Miss the Move of God

From the time Jesus began his public ministry until now, we should have been doing kingdom business. We cannot afford to take our kingdom assignment, position, or God-willed purpose for our lives lightly. We have been literally placed here so that we would save people from the works of darkness, as well as bring God's kingdom to earth. The kingdom of heaven is a steady and orderly advancement of Father God's plans in the earth. You may not see this advancement with your natural senses; however, with spiritual discernment, you will be able to recognize that there is a forward move taking place.

If no one else will dare to believe, we the children of God who have his seed within us should. We can no longer allow confusion, false teachings, or a pharisaical spirit to keep us away from God's truth that the kingdom of heaven has come. The hardness of the Pharisees' hearts along with a determination to do things their own way and not God's way kept them from advancing the kingdom of heaven. Like the Pharisees, we also must make a choice; either we are going to advance the kingdom of heaven or we are not. We need not be ignorant but realize that many would rather miss the move of God than change the way that they have been doing their own business.

The tradition of man and religion has always attempted to supersede the move of God. By allowing this, we have made the word and will of God of non-effect and have prevented the kingdom of heaven from being advanced as he has commanded. "Church" these days represents our culture and socialization more than the body of Christ or the kingdom of heaven. I believe, however, that we will get to a place where the true "church" (or ekklesia, which means "the called out ones") will do the work in which we were placed here to do (*Baker* 95). As we persistently pursue after Father God and his divine will; he will prepare us to reign in every sphere of influence in the world: relationships, family, education, government, media, arts, and finances. This is why it is so important that the mighty men and women of God daily spend time in the presence of the Father. Being in the presence of the Father, hearing his heart, and getting daily instructions will assure that we are positioned properly to advance the kingdom of heaven just as John and Jesus did.

Now that our spiritual eyes and hearts have been opened to the kingdom of heaven, there must be a transformation. When God gives revelation and illumination, he is giving us new perspectives on what he is doing and how he wants things done. This simply means that we cannot function in the same manner in which we have before or we will miss the move of God. Knowing this, there must be a change because God does not want us to remain the same. Just as John the Baptist was calling out in past times and saying, "Repent for the kingdom of heaven is at hand," the Spirit of God continues to call out today with the same message that the kingdom on heaven is at hand.

Jesus the Revolutionary; Our Example

I can understand why the words that Jesus spoke in St. Matthew 11:12 raise excitement for others, as well as for me . The words "suffereth violence and violent take it by force" are fighting words. They are radical, extreme, and revolutionary words. These words have the ability to cause the Spirit of God in you to rise up and assure you that you can do anything in Jesus' name. This scripture caused me to see Jesus as a revolutionary: a mover and shaker in the Spirit, someone that is relevant to the times, and that is all about doing kingdom business in a new and different way;a way that would draw people to the kingdom of heaven. Instead of using the law, he used love; instead of judgment, he used mercy. He instructed us to love our neighbor as ourselves, forgive so that we could receive forgiveness, give and it would be given back to us. These new principles and teachings of Jesus forcibly advanced, opened up the kingdom of heaven, and thereby gave us the opportunity to become a part of it.

Jesus' first account of being a revolutionary is when as a child he was left in Jerusalem by his parents, and they found him in the temple talking with the rabbis, the teachers of Jewish law.

The Bible says,

And it came to pass, that after three days they found him in the temple, sitting in the midst of the doctors, both hearing them, and asking them questions. And all that heard him were astonished at his understanding and answers. And when they saw him, they were amazed: and his mother said unto him, Son, why hast thou thus dealt with us? behold, thy father and I have sought thee sorrowing. And he said unto them, How is it that ye sought me? Wist ye not that I must be about my Father's business?

Luke 2:46–49

Jesus made it known to his earthly parents that he was on a mission from heaven. He knew who he was, what his purpose on the earth was, and where he was going. He knew that Father God had sent him to bring about a complete and radical change in the thinking and manner of living of his children. Jesus understood that it is God's desire that his children on earth know how the heavenly kingdom operates and how to follow suit, thereby, giving all mankind the opportunity to become part of the kingdom of heaven and to take back their rightful place of dominion.

Only a few chapters later we see the Lord after he has fasted for forty days and being tempted of the devil, defeated the devil and declared,

The Spirit of the Lord is upon me, because he hath anointed me to preach the gospel to the poor; he hath sent me to preach deliverance to the captives, and recovering of sight to the blind, to set at liberty them that are bruised, to preach the acceptable year of the Lord.

These words are kingdom words; they are full of action and power and reflect what true kingdom is all about. They are the epitome of what Jesus stands for and therefore what we should stand for. As I read these words that were spoken by Jesus years and years ago, I can still feel the *dunamis* (dynamite) power of the Holy Spirit that shatters and destroys every evil work of the devil. I am grateful that Jesus has not lost his power and he still has the same power today that he had over two thousand years ago.

There is no doubt that Jesus has taken the kingdom of heaven back for us; now it is time that we stop struggling, fight the good fight of faith, take hold of the promises of God, and advance the kingdom of heaven. The kingdom system has been established for us by our Father and helps us to work in harmony with his will. Therefore, when we are working in harmony with the Father, we will no doubt press into the kingdom of heaven and aggressively advance it by force in the spirit realm and see the manifestation of victory in the physical realm.

Knowing that there is no more time to struggle and what our purpose is, we must press into the kingdom of heaven and take it by force. We can no longer just be a hearer of the Word of God; we must become doers thereof. The Word of God is our substance and strength; it is the core of our lives and gives us the power and authority to rule and reign just as we were created to.

Chapter 3

WHAT ARE YOU CRYING FOR?

Knowing that we are pressing into the kingdom and taking it by force we must stop the crying and struggling and fight! I know that II Timothy 3:12 clearly states, "Yea, and all that will live godly in Christ Jesus shall suffer persecution," and Psalm 144:1 says, "Blessed be the Lord my strength, which teacheth my hands to war, and my fingers to fight." However, nowhere in the Bible have I found any scripture that supports the argument that it is okay for us to struggle.

Just Be Obedient!

Yes, there are many examples in the Bible where God's people suffered persecution and had to fight for what God promised them. One example is the renowned account of Moses' encounter with Pharaoh and the release of the Israelites from bondage, where they had been struggling in slavery for four hundred years. The Egyptians were fiercely pursuing and rapidly approaching the Israelites, and just as the children of Israel were between the Egyptian army and the Red Sea, Moses cried out to the Lord,

> And the Lord said unto Moses, Wherefore criest thou unto me? Speak unto the children of Israel, that they go forward: But lift thou up thy rod, and stretch out thine hand over the sea, and divide it: and the children of Israel shall go on dry ground through the midst of the sea.
>
> Exodus 14:15–16

Today God is asking us the same question that he asked Moses many years ago. Why are you crying to me? Open up your mouth and speak to every wayward situation, bringing them in submission to the Word of God while using the mighty name of Jesus. For I have given you everything you need to defeat and overthrow the army of the enemy. I have given you the Holy Spirit and authority to subdue and have dominion here on earth. Stop crying and do what I have instructed you to do.

Instead of being fearful and allowing our emotions to be in control, we must pull out the weapons that lay dormant within us. We must become doers of the Word of God, not just hearers and readers of it.

Ephesians 6:10–13 says,

... be strong in the Lord, and in the power of his might. Put on the whole armour of God, that ye may be able to stand against the wiles of the devil. For we wrestle not against flesh and blood, but against principalities, against powers, against the rulers of the darkness of this work, against spiritual wickedness in high places. Wherefore take unto you the whole armour of God, that ye may be able to withstand in the evil day, and having done all, to stand.

Many in the body of Christ, including me, realize that the only way we are going to defeat our enemy the devil is by following the specific instructions of Father God. We have been told that we are not fighting flesh and blood but spiritual wickedness and the powers of darkness, enemies that cannot be seen with the physical eye. Therefore, it would be foolish for us to think that we can be victorious in our flesh. Since God planned for us to have the victory, he has made it clear to us who we are fighting against and what weapons we need in our arsenal to defeat our enemy. Weapons such as truth, righteousness, peace, faith, salvation, and the Word of God. In addition to these weapons, God has given us instructions to pray, fast, and follow the Holy Spirit's guidance. God's weapons have been tried and proven to be detrimental against spiritual wickedness; therefore, they provide maximum damage to the kingdom of darkness. No longer can we cry out in fear. Like Moses, we also must learn to fight with what has been placed in our hands. We must be encouraged as we prepare for battle. For the victory has already been won!

No More Crying

The body of Christ recognizes that there has to be more to living from day to day where we do the same things, quote the same scriptures, and see no victory in our lives or in the lives of other believers. We don't desire to cry or struggle. We just have not had a clear understanding and revelation of God's Word. Some of us have been afraid to seek after the heart of God, his will, and his ways for ourselves. Therefore, we have eagerly looked to others for God's direction and instruction in our lives. No wonder we have struggled aimlessly, not knowing the way to go. Today, however, we can stop the struggling and crying as we start to seek God for ourselves.

I believe that we know what is required for an intimate relationship with Father God; however, we just have not been willing to go that far. Could it be our lack of knowledge and understanding about the spirit world? Maybe the strange and unknown have caused us to be afraid of going after God with our whole hearts; or maybe fear has nothing to do with it; could it just be our lack of commitment or just no desire to seek God? Perhaps we are just seeking after the Father for what he can give us. Whatever the reasons why we have not sought God, we have stopped the best that God has for our lives. Our physical eyes, as well as our spirit, witness daily to us and tell us that we are not receiving the promises and manifestations that the Word of God declares should be present in our lives.

Since God cannot lie, there has to be a problem with us. We simply must not be following the Father's instructions. Therefore, Jesus shows us how to stop the crying and struggling and shows us how to get what we need. In all his wisdom and splendor Jesus starts out by saying,

> Behold the fowls of the air: for they sow not, neither do they reap, nor gather into barns: yet your heavenly Father feedeth them. Are you not much better than they? Which of you by taking thought can add one cubit unto his statue? And why take ye thought for raiment? Consider the lilies of the field, how they grow; they toil not, neither do they spin: And yet I say unto you, that even Solomon in all his glory was not arrayed like one of these. Wherefore, if God so clothe the grass of the field, which today is, and tomorrow is cast into the oven, shall he not much more clothe you, O ye of little faith? Therefore, take no thought, saying what shall we eat? Or, What shall we drink? Or, Wherewithal shall we be clothed? (For after all these things do the Gentiles seek:) for your heavenly Father knoweth that ye have need of all these things. But seek ye first the kingdom of God, and his righteousness; and all these things shall be added unto you.
>
> Matthew 6:26–33

First, Jesus reminds us of birds and flowers of the field that depend on the Father for their daily existence just like us, which we so often overlook. Then he goes on to tell us that we are more important than any of the things that our Father has placed on earth to provide us with joy. Lastly, he tells us how to solve our dilemma of struggling and how to stop the crying. His instruction to us is to allow the Father's desires to become our desires and to seek after the kingdom of heaven. He knows that when we start seeking after the kingdom of heaven, we come in alignment with God's Word. This is where we align ourselves with the Father's heart and fulfill his will. Fulfilling God's will cause all of our needs to be met whether they are spiritual or natural. This is when the promises and the Word of God are manifested into the visible and God's kingdom or heavenly government comes to earth.

Jesus has made it very plain that we should not be anxious about anything because our God and Father is the creator and sustainer of all things; especially his children. We must simply trust, obey, and be in continual pursuit of the Father with all our hearts, minds, souls, and strength to attain all of what God declared for us from the foundation of the world.

We Have the Keys to the Kingdom

If we believe the Word of God to be true and to whom much is given much is required, then we must start to walk in all that Jesus has instructed us. If God and his Word are true, we have no other choice but to believe and declare that the kingdom of God has come. It was established on earth over two thousand years ago when Jesus rightfully took his place as the Son of God and walked this earth as an example to show us how the kingdom should work in the here and now. Then he died for our sins, was resurrected from the dead, and now is sitting on the right hand of the Father in heaven. At that time, Jesus gave us the keys to the kingdom of heaven. These are the only keys that give us legal power to defeat the enemy and accomplish what we have been created for, and that is dominion.

Jesus said prior to his death,

> And I will give unto thee the keys of the kingdom of heaven: and whatsoever thou shalt bind on earth shall be bound in heaven: and whatsoever thou shalt loose on earth shall be loosed in heaven.
>
> Matthew 16:18–19

These keys are the authority of the believer. They are the prayer of binding and loosing in the name of Jesus. They have been given to us for kingdom ruling and reigning and allow us to break every generational curse, stronghold, and obstacle that would try to prevent us from governing the affairs of the King and walking in victory. The keys of the kingdom of heaven unlock the power and authority of God in our lives here on earth and give us the power and authority to bind up or lock the power of the devil. They allow us to permit or prohibit on earth what God permits or prohibits in heaven.

Don't Move until You Hear from Him

As the body of Christ we have been empowered to rise up strong through the power of the Holy Spirit and pierce the darkness of religion and tradition as we walk in dominion. God has chosen us for a great work here on earth as a part of his extended kingdom and we cannot afford to allow religion, tradition or lack of knowledge to prevent us from doing what we have been instructed to do. We must fight and fight to win.

When King Saul, one of David's many enemies had been killed in battle, David finally is able to walk into his God ordained purpose as king. When the Philistines heard that David had been anointed king they decided to go up against him.

The Bible says,

> And David enquired of God, saying, Shall I go up against the Philistines? And wilt thou deliver them into thine hand? And the Lord said unto him, Go up; for I will deliver them into thine hand. So they came up to Baal Perazim; and David smote them there. Then David said, God hath broken in upon mine enemies by mine hand like the breaking forth of waters: therefore they call the name of that place Baal Perazim.
>
> 1 Chronicles 14:10–11

God allowed David to break through upon his enemies with his own hands like the mighty force of water suddenly and forcefully breaking through a levy. He allowed David to bombard, penetrate, and pass through, piercing his enemy.

David had not been allowed to struggle but to fight with confidence and tenacity when direction was sought. Our God is not a respecter of persons; just as he showed David how to defeat his enemy, he will show us how to defeat ours. It is important, however, that we don't overlook the most important thing that David did prior to making a move. He recognized where his help came from. He dared not move until he sought direction and guidance from God. We too must realize that our victory will only come by obeying Father God's instructions and strategies. First Chronicles 14:17 says, "And the fame of David went out into all the lands; and the Lord brought the fear of him upon all nations." God is waiting to get the glory out of each and every one of our lives so that he can bring back the fear of the Lord upon all nations.

God again declared in Isaiah 53:12,

> Therefore will I divide him a portion with the great, and he shall divide the spoil with the strong; because he hath poured out his soul unto death: and he was numbered with the transgressors; and he bore the sin of many, and made intercession for transgressors.

God has divided Jesus a portion with the great and Jesus is waiting to divide the spoil with the strong. How long will we wait to break through the enemy's barriers so that we can walk into all that God has ordained for us? What are you waiting for? As the soldiers of Christ, we must embrace the kingdom of heaven, use the keys of the kingdom of heaven, be empowered by the power of the Holy Spirit, break through and take the spoils of the enemy for our King. The Father has called us to "the place of breaking through" in the spirit and natural realm where there is no defeat, only victory if we dare to trust him and move forth in faith.

We must hold tightly to and complete what God has commissioned us to do; always being mindful that this is not our kingdom but our Father's. We have only been given permission to oversee it. As we are obedient to our Father, the responsibility of victory lies in his hands and not ours.

We can no longer afford to buy into the enemy's lies. No matter how the circumstances of life may surround us we must know and walk in the truth of the Word of God. We must realize that it's no time to struggle; it's time to fight for all that God predestined for us from the foundation of the world. It is time to have a life of dominion and authority. We must never forget, " ... from the days of John the Baptist until now the kingdom of heaven suffereth violence, and the violent take it by force" (St. Matthew 11:12).

Chapter 4

ADVANCING THE KINGDOM OF HEAVEN AND FIGHTING THE GOOD FIGHT OF FAITH

Will You Believe God?

Advancing the kingdom of heaven will require us to "Fight the good fight of faith ..."

(I Timothy 6:12). Paul used these words to caution Timothy, a young minister of the gospel, not to get caught up in the things of the world that would prevent him from keeping his responsibilities and trusting God with his whole heart. Paul informs Timothy that he was actively engaged in a war and that he must fight to protect and shield his faith from the daily affairs of life. Even though this charge was written over 2,000 years ago, the command is still very relevant and has not lost its value in our lives today. Fighting the good fight of faith still means exactly what it says! We must defeat, subdue, and destroy every enemy that challenge our belief in God. Faith in God has always been and will always be the only weapon that will assure us victory in our lives and the manifestations to the promises of God.

Knowing that faith is the very substance of a meaningful relationship with God, it is of the uttermost importance that our belief systems align with the truth of the Word of God. What would it take for you to trust Father God with all of your heart, mind, soul, and strength so that you could stop the struggle in your life and advance the kingdom of heaven? I don't know what it would take for you, but I do know that Father God has always made it possible for his children to place their full confidence and trust in him. During creation, the Father prepared the Garden of Eden, the perfect place for his children, that they need not worry or struggle for anything.

In this place all they had to do was to trust and obey. Today he offers us the same opportunity to simply trust and obey. God has not changed and he is faithful to perform all the promises that he has made to us. Being assured of this we can stand firm in our faith knowing that "God is not a man, that he should lie, neither the son of man, that he should repent: hath he said and shall he not do it? Or hath he spoken, and shall he not make it good" (Numbers 23:19). Understanding and believing that God cannot lie is our first line of defense against all that would try to tell us different. God's Word and integrity stands alone. When we are fully persuaded that our God alone is the only true and sovereign God, supreme in power and authority, and that he is the one " ... who quickened the dead, and called those things which be not as though they were." (Romans 4:17), we can then trust him to make what seems to be impossible possible, even if he has to call it into existence for us.

Fighting the good fight of faith is to never stop believing God no matter how violent the opposition is that we may have to face. It is a conscience decision and not an emotional decision to take God at his Word. Therefore, fighting the good fight of faith is learning to securely fasten ones trust in God. Simply put, it is fighting as we trust heaven. It is continuing to work hard and believe God while the victory is being won and the promise is being manifested. I have learned that having a strong foundation in the Word of God fosters wholehearted dependence in the Father. It builds our faith and causes us to enter into God's rest.

God's rest is a supernatural place that can only be accessed through pure and simple trust in Father God.

Hebrews 4:1–3 says,

Let us therefore fear, lest, a promise being left us of entering into his rest, any of you seem to come short of it [it meaning the promise]. For unto us was the gospel preached, as well as unto them: *but the word preached did not profit them, not being mixed with faith in them that heard it.* For we which have believed do enter into rest, as he said, As I have sworn in my wrath, if they shall enter into my rest: although the works were finished from the foundation of the world.

The Message Bible says,

For as long, then as that promise of resting in him pulls us on to God's goal for us, we need to be careful that we're not disqualified. We received the same promises as those people in the wilderness, but the promises didn't do them a bit of good because they didn't receive the promises with faith. If we believe, though, we'll experience that state of resting. But not if we don't have faith. Remember that God said, "Exasperated, I vowed, 'They'll never get where they're going, never be able to sit down and rest.'" God made this vow, even though he'd finished his part before the foundation of the world.

God is expecting us to believe his Word and enter into his divine rest, stop the struggle, and advance the kingdom of heaven, not to be like those of old that heard the gospel preached but chose not to mix it with faith.

The creator knows that we have bodies of flesh and that there will be days when we'll need to pick ourselves up, shake ourselves off, and get back in the fight of faith. It is not up to me to judge anyone when it comes to his or her level of faith. We all must question ourselves to see if we our receiving the promises of God and if are walking in our destiny. If we search our hearts and find that we have missed the mark along the way, we must then decide if it is due to a lack of faith. If a lack of faith is our challenge , we must do what is required to get our faith back and that is to get back into the Word of God because "… faith cometh by hearing, and hearing by the word of God" (Romans 10:17).

Surely God has placed a measure of faith in each and every one of us that is waiting to be developed. I believe that when we recognize the potential that is lying dormant within us because of a lack of faith, we will run to God's Word. This is where we will be built up in our most holy faith so that we are able to receive all that the Father has for us.

The Time Is Now

I love God because he is merciful, gracious, and longsuffering towards us. How painful it must be for Father God knowing that he has all the answers for our lives and that we do not trust him, the one that has given us our very lives. It is our Father's desire that we would trust him, cast all of our cares on him, and not struggle. We are so blessed to have another opportunity to listen closely, believe, and obey God for he is saying,

> …Today if ye will hear his voice, Harden not your hearts, as in the provocation, in the day of temptation in the wilderness: When your fathers tempted me, proved me, and saw my works forty years. Wherefore I was grieved with that genera-tion, and said, They do always err in their heart;

and they have not know my ways. So I sware in my wrath, They shall not enter into my rest. Take heed, brethren, lest there be in any of you an evil heart of unbelief, in departing from the living God.

Hebrews 3:7–12

We have seen some of the miraculous works of God just as the children of Israel did and have no excuse to walk in unbelief or unrest. However, if we are not careful to recognize the spirit of doubt and complaining we too will find ourselves walking in fear, unbelief, and disobedience. Not being able to "fight the good fight of faith" and therefore missing the move of God.

When we look at the errors of the children of Israel, it should cause us to confront ourselves and confess that we too have allowed the enemy to defeat us too long. Therefore, we no longer have the precious commodity of time on our side to walk in fear. Nor can we afford to go around the mountain of hopelessness, poverty, sickness, or lack of any longer. Because for some of us the forty-year mark of going around the mountain is fast approaching. If we are not careful, we too will find ourselves dying in the wildness of unbelief and not accomplishing our purpose and destiny here on earth. We really have no choice; we must die to our own desires and become obedient to our Father. As we cast down the spirit of doubt and any other spirit that is attempting to prevent us from believing God, we will see victory in our lives.

The Promise Is Only for the Courageous

Numbers 13:1–29 tells us that God instructed Moses to send twelve men to search out Canaan, the land that he promised to give to his children. When the men returned after spying out the land for forty days, all twelve reported that the land flowed with milk and honey. All twelve had seen the Jebusites, Hittites, and all the other "ites". All twelve had seen the walled cities, and all twelve had seen the giants in the land. Ironically only two of the twelve believed that God could give them the land that he promised. Caleb and Joshua had the faith and spiritual vision to see what God had promised and to agree with God no matter what they saw with their natural eyes. The Word of God declares, "And Caleb stilled the people before Moses, and said, Let us go up at once and possess it; for we are, well able to overcome it" (Numbers 13:30).

I know that it takes courage to stand on the Word of God and believe God when everyone and everything around you is saying something totally different than what the Word of God declares. I have been in that situation myself many times. It is crucial, however, to only obey God's voice and denounce all other voices and emotions. It is imperative that we start to operate in the same type of unshakable faith that Caleb and Joshua had. We must still ourselves, believe God, and go up at once and possess the land: for we are well able to take it! How much more should we be able to believe God and advance his kingdom when we have the Holy Spirit abiding within us?

The Promise Is Only for the Obedient

Caleb's ability to believe God and not struggle with unbelief took him to the next level in God. It is very powerful and reassuring to know that we can touch the heart of God as well as move the hand of God by simply trusting and obeying him. God approved of Caleb and Joshua's faith and obedience to follow him fully when others chose not to. Today there is much talk about going to the next level and not enough action; we must realize, however, that faith and obedience is the only key that will open the door to the next level.

> Surely they shall not see the land which I sware unto their fathers, neither shall any of them that provoked me see it: But my servant Caleb, because he had another spirit with him, and hath followed me fully, him will I bring into the land whereinto he went, and his seed shall possess it.
>
> Numbers 14:23–24

God honors and praises Caleb; he calls him his servant and declares that Caleb has another spirit, a spirit of obedience and faith in his God. Not only does God praise Caleb but also rewards Caleb by allowing him to enter into the promised land. God's blessing to Caleb doesn't stop there; he continues by making this a generational blessing. He promises Caleb that his seed shall possess the very land that he had believed God for. You see, when we "fight the good fight of faith," it allows us to take our generational seed into their wealthy place as well, a land flowing with milk and honey. It is a place of wholeness: spiritually, physically, mentally, financially, and relationally in the here and now, where we can walk in dominion and reign in the spiritual and physical realm together.

Faithful or Faithless: Both Are Powerful, Which Will You Be?

However, when we walk in unbelief and doubt as the ten unbelieving did, we find ourselves in error and out of the will of God. Being faithless is just as powerful as being full of faith; only it produces the opposite. Just as faith produces a harvest of blessing, unbelief produces a harvest of lack, a deficiency in all areas of one's life. It would be bad enough for someone to produce lack in his or her life but to cause another generation to live in lack would be even worse. This is what can happen to the seed of the unbeliever unless the spirit of unbelief is broken.

God agrees with whatever his children speak with their mouths whether it is in faith or unbelief. God tells Moses,

> Say unto them, As truly as I live, saith the Lord, as ye have spoken in mine ears, so will I do to you: Your carcases shall fall in this wilderness; and all that were numbered of you, according to your whole number, from twenty years old and upward,

which have murmured against me. Doubtless ye
shall not come into the land, concerning which
I sware to make you to dwell therein, save Caleb
the son of Jephunneh, and Joshua the son of Nun.
But your little ones, which ye said should be prey,
them will I bring in, and they shall know the land,
which ye have despised. But as for you, your carcases, they shall fall in this wilderness. And your
children shall wander in the wilderness forty years,
and bear your whoredoms, until your carcases be
wasted in the wilderness.

Numbers 14:28–33

Immediately God's children would start to eat
of the fruit of their lips. Not only would the ten
unbelieving spies receive a sentence of death, but
also they would cause a whole nation from the
age of twenty and above to die in the wilderness
because of their evil report of unbelief. Their words
became like a wildfire or rapid spreading disease.

Unbelief in God's Word still has the power
to curse our lives and the generations to come
because doubt and unbelief breed disobedience
towards God and his will. God has warned us of
the importance of believing and obeying him; he
has made it very clear that our lives, as well, as our
families' well-being is dependent upon us living by
faith. He continues to encourage us to fight the
good fight of faith by keeping a place in our heart,
mind, soul, and spirit where we acknowledge and
daily bow down to the supremacy of God, Jesus—
our Lord and Savior—and the Holy Spirit—our
Comforter and Guide.

Chapter 5

FAITH

F: Fighting *A*: As *I*: I *T*: Trust *H*: Heaven

Faith is pivotal to be a disciple of Christ. However, it has caused many in the body of Christ much grief. This is because we have not learned to take God at his Word. For the Word of God declares, "But without faith it is impossible to please him: for he that cometh to God must believe that he is, and that he is a rewarder of them that diligently seek him" (Hebrews 11:6).

Knowing that it is impossible to please God without faith, what other choice do we have as his disciples, but to live by faith as we have been instructed to do? God has given me an acronym for the word FAITH, and it is: *Fighting As I Trust Heaven.* I love this acronym because it is so powerful and full of action just like faith. The acronym Fighting As I Trust Heaven is plainly another way that the Father is instructing us to trust him as we resist the devil, defend, and take back what belongs to us. Has our faith not been given to us for the purposes of ruling, reigning, and walking in dominion? Then, we must walk in faith in order to win.

Faith requires action on our part to be activated. Faith is a producer of things and is not stagnant. It is not passive or inactive but it is living, energetic, and vigorous, as well as supernatural. When one is operating in faith they do not stop from their daily activities of life, which include physical labor. Just the opposite; you become more engaged in seeking God for the direction that you need to take in order to walk out your promise and dreams. Yes, living by faith means that many times we will be required to use our natural hands and feet to defeat the devil and accomplish the will of God. For example, some of us will have to physically go into the marketplace with our gifts, talents, monies, and materials, as well as the gospel; thereby, putting our faith to work as we reach out with our hands and words and touch those that we come in contact with. This in turn will spread the good news about the love of Christ that many may believe and produce a mighty army that will subdue the land and walk in dominion for the cause of Christ. A working faith for others will include simply sitting down and putting their ideas on a piece of paper while believing God to give them the next steps toward fulfilling their dreams. Fighting as I trust heaven is all about becoming an instrument in the hands of God.

Faith without Works Is Dead!

Only faith and works being motivated by the love of God will produce the manifestations of the promises of God and advance the kingdom of heaven.

James 2:14–26 says,

> What doth it profit, my bretheren, though a man say he hath faith, and have not works? Can faith save him? If a brother or sister be naked, and destitute of daily food, And one of you say unto them, Depart in peace, be ye warned and filled; notwithstanding ye give them not those things which are needful to the body; what doth it profit? Even so faith, if it hath not works, is dead, being alone. Yea, a man may say, Thou hast faith, and I have works: show me thy faith without works, and I will show thee my faith by my works. Thou believest that there is one God; thou doest well: the devils also believe, and tremble. But wilt thou know, O vain man, that faith without works is dead? Was not Abraham our father justified by works, when he had offered Isaac his son upon the altar? Seest thou how faith wrought with his works, and by works was faith made perfect? And the scripture was fulfilled which saith, ABRAHAM BELIEVED GOD, AND IT WAS IMPUTED UNTO HIM FOR RIGHTEOUSNESS: and he was called the Friend of God. Ye see then how that by works a man is justified, and not by faith only. Likewise also was not Rahab the harlot justified by works, when she had received the messengers, and had sent them out another way? For as the body

without the spirit is dead, so faith without works
is dead also.

Could it be that we have not seen the promises
of God come to pass in our lives because we have
failed to mix faith and works together? Or maybe
it is because we have only been concerned about
ourselves and not about how we could be a blessing to someone else.

I can hear some of you now saying, "How dare
she say that we must work for our salvation." By
no means am I speaking of one having to work for
their salvation. Ephesians 2:8–9 clearly states, "For
by grace are ye saved through faith; and that not of
yourselves: it is a gift of God; Not of works, lest any
man should boast." I am specifically talking about
giving God something to work with when it comes
to believing for your dreams and those things that
God has promised you. Abraham was required of
God to offer his son, and it was accounted to him
as righteousness and he became the father of faith.
Father God also offered his only begotten son that
we may have everlasting life. In turn, we became
the children of God through Christ and heirs to
the promise that was made to Abraham. "And if
ye be Christ's, then are ye Abraham's seed, and
heirs according to the promise" (Galatians 3:29). If
we believe the Bible, which is the epitome of the
kingdom of heaven, we must follow suit and give
God something to work with as well. Faith that
causes one to work is as important as believing and
receiving the manifestation from God itself.

Use What's In Your Hands So the Impossible
Can Come to Pass!

Another example of faith and works benefiting from each other is captured in 1 Kings 17. Here the prophet Elijah has been instructed by God to go to Zaraphath where God has divinely prepared a means of survival for him and another family during a famine in the land. Elijah, already being notified by God, journeys to the place where God commanded him, and there a widow supplies him with food . When Elijah arrives and sees the widow, he asks her first for a drink of water. As she is going to get the water, he then asks her for a piece of bread. The woman replies to Elijah that all she has is a small amount of meal and oil that she is getting ready to prepare so that she and her son can eat it and die. Elijah, already knowing the mind and will of God, encourages the woman not to be fearful but to go and prepare the bread as she had planned. He instructs her, to make a portion for him first and bring it to him, then to go back and prepare the bread for herself and her son. Elijah tells the widow that if she will do exactly what he asked of her that the Lord God of Israel said,

> The barrel of meal shall not waste, neither shall the cruse of oil fail, until the day that the Lord sendeth rain upon the earth. And she went and did according to the saying of Elijah: and she, and he, and her house, did eat many days. And the barrel of meal wasted not, neither did the cruse of oil fail, according to the word of the Lord, which he spake by Elijah.
>
> 1 Kings 17:14–16

When the widow had been asked by Elijah to prepare him a piece of bread, I am sure as a mother that she was not concerned about his needs. At this dismal time of her life, she was probably only interested in the well-being of her son as she planned to prepare their last meal and die. I do not know if the widow understood the principle, faith without works is dead. Did she have a full under-standing how God would supernaturally provide for her and her child? I seriously doubt it. I do believe, however, that she realized that God was requiring her to take a step of faith and that meant using what was in her hand. As she moved in faith and obedience, she was able to reap the blessings of God and see the impossible come to pass.

We Need Each Other

Faith requires help from others many times. Elijah, full of faith and knowing the will and plans of God, tells the Zarephath widow not to fear but only have faith and obey. When one can see through the eyes of faith it is truly enlightening because it causes us to come out of spiritual and natural dark-ness. When we are in spiritual or natural darkness, we often suffer loss or can be completely destroyed. This could have been the fate of the widow if she had not had help to believe. I have come to real-ize that the longer I live by faith the more I need others in my life. The survival of Elijah and this family was dependent upon each other. Elijah had to believe that he was hearing from God and then obey and the woman had to believe that Elijah had heard from God and also obey. There is no doubt in my heart that we need each other like never before.

As I look around, little by little, I can see the world's system attempting to chip away at our foundation of faith. Someone is always trying to get God out of our lives. Therefore, we must help our generations continue to know who our God is and what he can do as they see us walking in faith. It is important that we leave a legacy of faith along with the testimonies of what our great God did for us. I believe that this will unequivocally allow them to stand up and tell the world what their God can and will do and then have the signs and wonders to follow. Not only do we need one another's testimonies, but we also need to be in agreement with one another as we believe. The prayer of agreement is one of the most powerful and important prayers that can be prayed. It is a prayer with a promise when faith and harmony come together. The promise is " ... That if two of you shall agree on earth as touching anything that they shall ask, it shall be done for them of my Father which is in heaven" (Matthew 18:19). God has not called us on this journey alone but has given us helpers and encouragers along the way. Why not reach out and help someone? I believe that someone is waiting to reach back and help you.

God Wants the Best for Us

Whether in good times or bad, we must always remember that our God is more than enough for whatever challenges that may come our way and he wants the best for us. God has always desired that we would prosper and be in health. Third John 2 says, "Beloved, I wish above all things that thou mayest prosper and be in health, even as thy soul prospereth." I don't believe that God can make it any clearer than this scripture that he wants the best for us. When God's children take the time to know his heart, mind, and will, then we are able to believe him. Confidence in God will only come by spending quality time in his presence where intimacy and fellowship will be formed. Then there will be no doubt that God desires that we have wealth. Isn't money the way that he prospered the Zarephath widow?

Not only does God desire wealth for us, he also desires that we walk in health. Wealth and health belong together. What good is there to have wealth and not have the health to spend some of it? On the other hand, what good is there to have health and no wealth to spend? Like the widow, he has placed something in each and every one of our hands that he may prosper us also. It is up to us to earnestly seek him to find out what is in our hands. Once we have done that we can trust and obey him to multiply it.

Let us never forget that God has always been concerned about every integral part of man and knows that our wholeness depends upon our faith in him. He has always been and always will be our only source of wholeness. Therefore, we must come to the realization that *our faith* is the key that will enable us to prosper in every area of our lives. Yes, even in our most inner being: where the core of whom we are and where true prosperity always begins. Let's continue to fight as we trust heaven because his kingdom has come and the struggle is over.

F: *Fighting* A: *As* I: *I* T: *Trust* H: *Heaven*

Chapter 6

SEEING WHAT GOD SEES

I will stand upon my watch, and set me upon the tower, and will watch to see what he will say unto me, and what I shall answer when I am reproved. And the Lord answered me, and said, Write the vision, and make it plain upon tables, that he may run that readeth it. For the vision is yet for an appointed time, but at the end it shall speak, and not lie: though it tarry wait for it; because it will surely come, it will not tarry. Behold, his soul which is lifted up is not upright in him: but the just shall live by his faith.

Habakkuk 2:1–4

When God spoke these words to Habakkuk, he knew that they would be an inspiration to us just as they had been for Habakkuk and the people of his day. God in his sovereignty was well aware that we would see days of violence, unrighteousness, and all sorts of economical upheaval just as during the days that Habakkuk penned these words. He knew that we too would desire to have an understanding regarding what to expect in the days to come. Therefore, as an example, he uses the same words that he spoke to Habakkuk to let us know that he will answer pray and send clarity.

God's answer to Habakkuk kept his people from losing heart. Today it is still God's answers to prayer that keeps us from losing heart. God's desire is that we don't lose faith but just trust him and see what he is seeing. As we continue to seek God as Habakkuk did, we too will receive supernatural revelations knowledge and discernment for our times. Our God is faithful and just. Just as he had a divine plan and purpose for the people of Habakkuk's time, I know without a doubt that he has one for us. Don't fret; be assured that no matter what it takes, our God will send clarity. It may come through his word, the prophetic, prayer, or even a vision, but clarity will come. Our God will never fail us. Father God has always wanted us to know his will for our lives and the generations to come. He knows that our very existence is dependent upon him. Therefore, he has always had a watchman on the wall; someone that would watch to see what he would say. Someone that he could show his will to for his people.

Even though nations may be shaking all around us, as God's people, we have no reason to be fearful because the kingdom of our God is not of this world. Our confidence must continue to stand firmly in God and his Word knowing that he will show us what we need to do to walk in victory. Therefore, it is time for us to see what God is seeing and do great exploits for our King. Habakkuk's words continue to ring forth to encourage us that no matter what type of mayhem we may be facing, the just must live by faith while awaiting the manifestations of his promises.

We Must Be Dreamers and Visionaries

What is holding you back from becoming the dreamer or visionary that God has called you to be? What has locked up your desire to go where you have never gone before? Whatever it may have been I encourage you not to allow it to hold you back any longer. God is waiting to make what may seem impossible come to reality in our lives.

First Corinthians 2:9–14 says,

> But as it is written, Eye hath not seen, nor ear heard, neither have entered into the heart of man, the things which God hath prepared for them that love. But God hath revealed them unto us by his Spirit: for the Spirit searcheth all things, yea, the deep things of God… Now we have received, not the spirit of the world, but the spirit which is of God; that we might know the things that are freely given to us of God… But the natural man receiveth not the things of the Spirit of God: for they are foolishness unto him: neither can he know them, because they are spiritually discerned.

When we are able to see what God is seeing it allows us to have a greater understanding of who we are in him, those things that belong to us, as well as, how to apprehend them by faith. Dreams and visions let us look into the future and can allow us see what God has predestined for us. These audiovisual means of communication from the Father can actually give clarity and directions for our lives and prevent us from being defeated by our enemies. There is no doubt that the vision or foresight of God is a necessity for his people today, just as it was in the days of old.

God continues to declare,

> And it shall come to pass in the last days, ... I will pour out of my spirit upon all flesh: and your sons and your daughters shall prophesy, and your young men shall see visions, and your old men shall dream dreams: And on my servants and on my handmaidens I will pour out in those days of my spirit; and they shall prophesy.

Acts 2:17

What are you waiting for? Allow God to pour out of his spirit upon you today. These supernatural manifestations will help us to discern the true nature of a situation and give us God's continual guidance and provision, causing us to be positioned steps ahead of our opponents.

God gave us what is required to be a visionary over 2,000 years ago when Jesus got up out of the grave with all power in his hands. Jesus' triumph became our triumph removing all boundaries that kept us from having and being all that God intended . His intent from the very beginning of time until now was that we would see that we were created to rule and reign just as he planned from the foundation of the world. This is why it is so important for us to understand that "Where there is no vision, the people perish ..." (Proverbs 29:18). Literally, when there is no insight or spiritual light available to show us the will of God we become a destitute and despondent people without destiny or hope. However, when we see what God is seeing, we are not just fighting against the air; we are like a missile that has been locked onto its target that cannot miss.

It should be sobering for us to know that God always had plans for us. He has placed the dreams and inspirations that we have deep down within us. For he said, "'For I know the plans that I have for you,' declares the Lord, 'Plans to prosper you not to harm you, plans to give you hope and a future'" (Jeremiah 29:11, NIV).

God's blueprints for each and every one of our lives have been divinely orchestrated. Before we were even a thought in our parents' minds, he knew exactly which ways we would take. God has always had the best on his mind when it came to his children. He has never had any intentions to hurt us; only to bless us and show forth his glory through each and every one of us, as we are able to see what the Father is seeing.

May the Eyes of Your Understanding Be Enlightened

The illumination and comprehension of God's Word will cause us to pray for others and ourselves just as Paul prayed for us many years ago:

> That the God of our Lord Jesus Christ, the Father of glory, may give us the spirit of wisdom and revelation in the knowledge of him: The eyes of your understanding being enlightened; that ye may know what is the hope of his calling, and what the riches of the glory of his inheritance in the saints. And what is the exceeding greatness of his power to us-ward who believe, according to the working of his mighty power, which he wrought in Christ, when he raised from the dead, and set him at his own right hand in the heavenly places. Far above all principality, and power, and might, and dominion, and every name that is named, not only in this world, but also in that which is to come: And hath put all things under his feet, and gave him to be the head over all things to the church, Which is his body, the fullness of him that filleth all in all.
>
> Ephesians 1:17–23

Paul knew that the opening of our spiritual eyes would bring clear understanding of what was true and lasting. Once we really know who our Father is and how much he loves us, we can partake of all the great things that he has planned for us. I believe that Paul knew that as the scales of tradition and religion fall off of our eyes, we would be able to see just as God sees and just as Adam had seen in the Garden of Eden before the fall.

Paul was certain that just as his eyes were opened, our eyes would be opened and our purpose and destiny would be revealed to us. He knew then that no devil in hell could prevent us from answering the call, walking in dominion, and embracing the truth about the kingdom of God once revelation had come. Paul knew the power of prayer and realized that we must not only pray but ask the Holy Spirit to give us true revelation of who Jesus is, what he did for us as he walked this earth, and why he died on the cross and rose from the grave with all power in his hand.

Knowing that it is God's desire that the eyes of our understanding be enlightened, we cannot take seeing what God sees as a small matter. Especially since *seeing what God sees* is all about getting divine direction and guidance from the Father and fulfilling our purpose and destiny here on earth.

Chapter 7

OUR HELPER IN THE FIGHT

Our Helper Is Here

As the world face all kinds of uncertainty and struggle to figure out what they need to do to survive the mayhem, God continues to assure his children that he has sent us help; so we need not struggle. Our helper is none other than the Holy Spirit, which is the Spirit of God. He is the one that Jesus asked his Father to send to us prior to his ascension back to heaven. Yes, he is the one that has been given to us to lead and guide us into all truth.

As I walk and mature in the truth of God's Word, I have come to the realization that I do not have the answers to solve all of my problems alone. I now know that it is wise to seek help from others, especially the Holy Spirit. I'll never forget the day that I was seeking answers from the Lord when very clearly the Holy Spirit spoke to me. In his own distinct way, he let me know that if I was willing to fight that he would fight for me and with me. That day, God, through his Spirit, reinforced his will for me to be victorious in every area of my life. He let me know that I had the Holy Spirit assisting me in the fight for all he had purposed for me from the foundation of the world. No longer did I have to worry; now all Ihave to do is to follow the lead and guidance of his Spirit.

The Holy Spirit: A Gift. Will You Receive Him?

I have always thought that everyone enjoyed receiving gifts. However, I have found out that this isn't true, especially when it comes to the gift of the Holy Spirit. Every day God attempts to give the gift of his Spirit, and every day many continue to refuse him. Why would someone be so willing to refuse one of the greatest gifts that could ever be given to man? Could it be that we do not realize the importance of this gift? Or perhaps we don't feel worthy of the gift? Whatever your reasoning may be for not accepting God's gift—the Holy Spirit—it is one of the worst decisions that could ever be made by God's children. Today I encourage you to ask the Father for the gift of the Holy Spirit if you haven't received him.

Jesus said,

> If a son shall ask bread of any of you that is a father, will he give him a stone? Or if he ask a fish, will he for a fish give him a serpent? Or if he shall ask an egg, will he offer him a scorpion? If you then, being

evil, know how to give good gifts unto your children: how much more shall your heavenly Father give the Holy Spirit to them that ask him?

Luke 11:11–13

As the children of God we must purposely open our hearts and spirits to receive the ministry of the Holy Spirit because he desires to help us. He has been sent to us from the Father to lead and guide us in the way that we should go. Ultimately, he helps us to be all that God desires for us to be. Therefore, we cannot be like the world, which does not believe that the Holy Spirit exist because they cannot see him and are unable to receive him as their God-sent helper. Ephesians 4:30 teaches, " … Grieve not the holy Spirit of God, whereby ye are sealed unto the day of redemption." Through this scripture, Father God has given us specific instruction not to grieve his Spirit because his Spirit testifies that we belong to him and are his ambassadors. The Holy Spirit is our helper and is multifaceted. One of his functions is to help keep us from being spotted by this world until we have been presented back to the Father.

He Can Only Help You if You Let Him

I thank God that he changes not. The identical ministry of the Holy Spirit, which the disciples received in biblical times, is readily available today for those that will ask the Father in Jesus' name. The Holy Spirit has been mandated by Father God to train us according to the prototype of the kingdom of heaven. Kingdom training will enable us to stop the struggle and do the King's business in the earth like we were instructed to do from the beginning of time. Unfortunately, until we have learned to yield to the Holy Spirit's instruction and guidance, we will continue to struggle. In order to stop the struggle and conduct kingdom business, there first must be order in our lives. God is not a God of disorder, so this means that we cannot be people of disorder. Once order has been achieved in our lives, we will be able to reign in the things of God. Could this be why we have not gone to the next level? If it is, then we need to willingly submit to God's supreme authority and power that abides in the person of the Holy Spirit so that he can equip us for kingdom business. Complete submission to the Spirit of God will always assure us that we are walking in our purpose and destiny.

Many of us have become so accustomed to functioning in this world's system and doing things our own way that we have been out of order and not even known it. Therefore, we must be mindful that our Helper's commitment and responsibility to us becomes void if we choose not to obediently follow his instructions. We must never forget that the spirit of self-reliance and independence is what caused the struggle from the beginning. We can get the help that we need by allowing the power of the Holy Spirit to live in and through us. As children of the King, we have no excuses for failure if we receive the Holy Spirit and allow him to lead and guide us. For we have been given the awesome opportunity to be empowered and filled by the selfsame power that raised Jesus out of the grave, our Comforter and Helper; the Spirit of the true and living God.

The Holy Spirit, Our Guide to Truth

Many times we say that we want to know the truth about ourselves, as well as what the will of God is for our lives; however, deep down within, we really don't want to. Maybe it is because when we know the truth, we will be required to do better. Regardless of our shortcomings, the Holy Spirit, which is also known as the Spirit of Truth, has come to help us walk in truth.

Jesus said,

> Howbeit when he, the Spirit of truth, is come, he will guide you into all truth: for he shall not speak of himself, but whatsoever he shall hear, that shall he speak: and he will shew you things to come. He shall glorify me: for he receive of mine, and shall shew it unto you. All things that the Father hath are mine: therefore said I, that he shall take of mine, and shall shew it unto you.
>
> St. John 16:13–15

The Holy Spirit wants us not only to walk in truth about ourselves but also regarding the kingdom of God and what God is presently doing and going to do in the future. He wants to set our inner man free from all that would try to bind us up, as well as give us a greater understanding about God's kingdom.

Just as Jesus had been an active part of his disciples' lives and imparted truth to them about the kingdom of heaven, he knew that we too would need someone to teach us. He was confident that the Spirit of truth would help us to be victorious and would teach us just as he had taught his disciples. Jesus knew that the Spirit of truth would not speak of himself but only of the one that he had been sent to glorify. Walking in the Spirit of truth is powerful because it is one way that we can defeat the devil. Therefore, we must allow the Spirit of truth to search our inward parts and reveal those things that may also be keeping us away from the best that the Father has for us. Prayerfully, this will cause us to confess any sin or disobedience that may be causing strong holds and destruction and in our lives. Since the Spirit of truth has been given to us to lead and guide us into all truth, let us therefore, follow his lead because we have not been this way before and he knows the way that we should take. Our Father has given him specific directions for each and everyone of our lives.

Holy Spirit, Our Comforter

I am now at a place in my life where I need a comforter. I can remember the times when I felt that I didn't need anyone to comfort me or encourage me. I thought that I could handle whatever life brought my way. However, I have come to realize that only a fool or someone full of pride would resist the comfort of others, especially that of Holy Spirit, our Comforter. Jesus the Son of God even needed to be comforted when he was in the Garden of Gethsemane. What makes us think that we don't need the comfort and encouragement of someone else? I believe as Christians we have put on facades for so long that we have forgotten who we really are. We have forgotten that we are helpers one to another and that we need each other. Today I want to encourage you that it's okay to receive the comfort of your brothers and sisters in Christ and that especially of the Holy Spirit, our Comforter. There is no need that you walk alone.

Jesus understood that we would need comforting because our hearts would grow weary at times. Thankfully, he is very compassionate and concerned about us that he doesn't want us to be afraid or troubled about the cares of this world. He was so considerate that he prayed to his Father. His actual words were, "And I will pray the Father, and he shall give you another Comforter, that he may abide with you forever" (John 14:16). Because of this prayer, the Holy Spirit, our Comforter, has come to live in us. He is the one that gives us peace that passes all understanding and whose quiet, still voice we hear many times. Our Comforter, the Holy Spirit, daily prompts or unction us so that we will know the direction that we should take. Father God has equipped us with all that we need.

God sent his Son and his Son sent the Holy Spirit, our Comforter. Now it is time that we stop struggling; walk in our purpose and destiny, so that our Father's will can be done on earth as it is in heaven.

Chapter 8

I WON'T KEEP SILENT ANY LONGER!

I Have Got to Open My Mouth

To everything there is a season, and a time to every purpose under the heaven: A time to be born, and a time to die; a time to plant, and a time to pluck up that which is planted; A time to kill, and a time to heal; a time to break down, and a time to build up; A time to weep, and a time to laugh; a time to mourn, and a time to dance; a time to cast away stones, and a time to gather stones together; a time to embrace, and a time to refrain from embracing; a time to get, and a time to lose; a time to keep, and a time to cast away; A time to rend, and a time to sew; a time to keep silence, *and a time to speak.*

Ecclesiastes 3:1–7

What potent and articulate words this writer uses to express his thoughts. King Solomon, heir of King David, the son of Bath-sheba, penned these very insightful yet somewhat poetic words. The wisest man that has ever lived starts out by proclaiming the significance of seasons and times. Seasons and times are words that are synonyms or have some type of similarity. Both suggest a period of life that may be right or fitting for someone or something to make a change, do something different, or go to the next level. Seasons and times have the ability to catapult you forward if seized at the appropriate time or cause you to remain in a holding position until the next opportunity avails itself; they are like keys to opening or locking doors and can be indicative of success or failure. Solomon continues by advising us that seasons and times influence every destination, goal, assignment, aspiration and every purpose on earth. Then immediately, he begins to encourage us by letting us know that whatever life experience we might be facing, whether favorable or not as favorable, with time it will change.

Knowing that the kingdom of heaven has come is a favorable time for the body of Christ. It is a time that we can advance God's kingdom by walking in our purpose and destiny. It is also the time and season for us to boldly witness of God's goodness and mercy to the lost. Most of all, it is time for us to open up our mouths and declare in faith the promises of God and the will of God over our lives, as well as the lives of our loved ones. There is no time like the present that we start speaking to every obstacle that has held us back and demand that they let us go. While we continue to declare the blessings of God and see them come to pass. Jesus has given us authority to speak to any situation and bring about a change if we are able to believe.

He continues to tell us to:

> Have faith in God. For verily I say unto you, That whosoever shall say unto this mountain, Be thou removed, and be thou cast into the sea; and shall not doubt in his heart, but shall believe that those things which he saith shall come to pass; he shall have whatsoever he saith. Therefore I say unto you, What things soever ye desire, when ye pray, believe that ye receive them, and ye shall have them.
>
> Mark 11:23–24

Jesus has let me know that the fate of my life is in my mouth. Therefore, I have no choice. I have got to open my mouth and speak in faith the promises of God. I can't be silent any longer, and neither can you.

An Instrument of Life or Death

I especially love the scripture that talks about "a time to keep silent, and a time to speak" because it's one that I can relate to. Most people that know me know that I enjoy a good conversation. To be perfectly honest, I have had many occasions where

I should have kept silent, didn't and I simply failed the "quiet game." Thanks be to our God that he is a God of a second, third, fourth, and ... time. (Se'lah!)

I have learned that in God's kingdom there must be self-control in everything that we do especially when it comes to our speech. Our tongues have gotten many of us out of the will of God. Not to speak of generations and generations of families who have been cursed because of words that they have spoken or someone else have spoken over them.

James 3:2–10 says,

> For in many things we offend all. If any man offend not in word, the same is a perfect man, and able also to bridle the whole body. Behold, we put bits in the horses' mouths, that they may obey us; and we turn about their whole body. Behold also the ships, which though they be so great and are driven of fierce winds, yet are they turned about with a very small helm, whithersoever the governor listeth. Even so the tongue is a little member, and boasteth great things. Behold, how great a matter a little fire kindleth! And the tongue is a fire, a world of inquity: so is the tongue among our members, that it defileth the whole body, and setteth on fire the course of nature; and it is set on fire of hell. For every kind of beasts, and of birds, and of serpents, and of things in the sea, is tamed, and hath been tamed of mankind: But the tongue can no man tame; it is an unruly evil, full of deadly poison. Therewith bless we God, even the Father; and therewith curse we men, which are made after the similitude of God. Out of the same mouth proceedeth blessing and cursing. My brethren, these things ought not so to be.

It is amazing how these words that were written over thousands of years ago speak so clearly to us in the new millennium. It is as though we are looking in a mirror of past times and see ourselves as we are today.

Many times I have come face to face with these scriptures because of the correction of the Holy Ghost. Immediately the condemnation of the enemy would show me my inadequacies, cause me to want to be silent and not to speak another word. I realize just how resistant and disorderly the tongue can be, but to be silent is not the answer. Learning the power and effects of the spoken word and then changing the way that we use words is our remedy for this problem.

Words are capable of transcending time like a bullet or boomerang piercing our very souls when spoken inappropriately. Whether it is God's Word, ours, or someone else's, they have the ability to produce life or death. Solomon said, "A man's belly shall be satisfied with the fruit of his mouth; and with the increase of his lips shall he be filled. Death and life are in the power of the tongue: and they that love it shall eat the fruit thereof" (Proverbs 18:20–21). According to Solomon, words give authority, jurisdiction, and dominion over every situation in our lives. We can find ourselves full or famished by whatever we allow to proceed out of our mouths. Solomon explains that unskillful words can literally cause one to be destitute, barren, and live in lack when we refuse to align our speech with the Word of God. On the other hand, when we choose to speak in agreement and in harmony with God, we will find ourselves living a life of abundance and prosperity; where more than enough is our portion. However, we choose to employ our words will produce life or death whether it is in the spiritual or physical realm.

Declaration of the Word of God along with faith and obedience is essential for kingdom living. It will keep us focused, assist us in fulfilling our purpose and destiny, stop us from struggling, and encourage us to fight the good fight of faith. When we believe and declare the Word of God, it is established deep within our hearts and minds. It becomes a sword in our mouths, sets the atmosphere or attitude for victory, and allows us to refute every lie of the devil.

When we don't, however, see through the devil's vices of deception and speak anything that comes to mind or choose not to speak God's Word over our challenges, we give the enemy authority to bring those things to pass. Recognizing the devil's tactics and schemes enables us to resist every foul, foolish, and unskilled word that can be used against us. Knowing that there is power in the spoken word and that the same creative power in which God used to speak this world into existence abides in our mouths, by the power of the Holy Spirit, we must always be mindful of the words that we allow to flow out of our mouths.

Activate the Word So That God Can Activate the Heavens

With the very words of our mouths, we have the ability to take immediate possession of kingdom victories that are hanging in the balance and bring forth an extraordinary kingdom harvest. As we literally go into the enemy's camp and take back what he has taken from us; whether it is spiritual, physical, financial, mental, or relational. When Jesus spoke to Peter, he said,

> And I say also unto thee, That thou art Peter, and upon this rock I will build my church; and the gates of hell shall not prevail against it. And I will give unto thee the keys of the kingdom of heaven: and whatsoever thou shalt bind on earth shall be bound in heaven: and whatsoever thou shalt loose on earth shall be loosed in heaven.
>
> Matthew 16:18–19

Simply put, Jesus instructed Peter to activate the Word of God so that God could activate the heavens. Today Jesus continues to instruct us to activate the Word of God because God continues to await the opportunity to activate his Word. Isaiah 51:16 echoes this same thought; it says, "And I have put my words in thy mouth, and I have covered thee in the shadow of mine hand, that I may plant the heavens, and lay the foundations of the earth, and say unto Zion, Thou art my people." Because we are God's people he has put his words into our mouths that we would speak into the atmosphere and cause his will to be established on the earth that he would be glorified. We must learn to take the scriptures and make them personally ours because they are. God has given us the power to speak those things that are not, into being as we align our words with his words.

In Luke 1:38 the angel Gabriel tells Mary that she will be the mother of the Savior of the world. Mary responds and says, "Behold the handmaid of the Lord; be it unto me according to thy word." Immediately after reading this scripture, the Holy Spirit spoke to me and said, "Be it unto you according to your word." He was letting me know that I have to power to decree a thing, and it shall come to pass. Therefore, we must stop looking and waiting for others to speak into our lives. If the Word of God is in our mouths, we must start to decree it over our families and ourselves and watch what we say come to pass.

When we declare the Word of God in faith, we are taking ownership of what God said that we could have. We are literally bringing God's Word back to his remembrance and therefore putting a demand on him.

Thus saith the Lord, the Holy One of Israel, and his Maker, Ask me of things to come concerning my sons, *and concerning the work of my hands command ye me.* I have made the earth, and created man upon it: I, even my hands, have stretched out the heavens, and all their host have I commanded.

Isaiah 45:11–12

God has given us permission to command him and I know no other way but through his Word. How can we keep silent any longer? We must open our mouths and speak the Word of God in faith. Thereby giving God and his heavenly host the awesome opportunity to accomplish every word that we have decreed in Jesus' name. So let's start decreeing now.

Father, in the name of Jesus, I make the quality decision to take control of my tongue. I renounce, reject, and repent of every word I have spoken against you and your operation in life. I cancel the power of those words and dedicate my tongue to speaking your word. Out of the abundance of the heart, the mouth speaks, so I set myself to fill my heart with your word. Put a watch, oh Lord, over my lips. I set myself to speak in line with the word. As your child, I confess that I am healed, I am filled with your mighty Holy Spirit, I am the righteousness of God through Jesus Christ, I am victorious in every area of my life, because you have made it so. Father, I thank you that I no longer will be double-minded by the words of my mouth. I let the word of Christ dwell in me richly in all wisdom. Everything I do, whether in word or deed, I do in the name of the Lord Jesus Christ giving thanks unto you. In Jesus' name, amen!

Author unknown

Chapter 9

THE CAPACITY ENLARGER

Tapping into the Wisdom of God

Some years ago, we heard people using the slang term "living large." For the most part, the term meant that someone was doing exceptionally well economically and that it seemed as though they had everything together when it came to the material things of life. Regardless of how they had gotten the nice cars, the big house, the fancy clothes, or the money in the bank, we gave them all kinds of accolades. Many of us thought and continue to think that this is the way to go because we desire to *live large* also. Don't get me wrong; I have no problems with material things and would be the first to tell you to go for the gold. However, for me I have come to the truth of what *living large* is. Living large is tapping into the wisdom of God and obediently following the instructions that I have been given. I have also found that wisdom is the capacity enlarger of every area of our lives, which means that you won't need to worry about trying to *live large* on your own because wisdom will show you just what you need to do.

Right about now you probably want to know more about wisdom. Well, this is what she has to say about herself. Yes, that is right. The Bible speaks of wisdom with female connotations.

Wisdom is powerful, and this is what she has to say:

The Lord possessed me in the beginning of his way, before his works of old. I was set up from everlasting, from the beginning, or ever the earth was. When there were no depths, I was brought forth; when there were no foundations abounding with water. Before the mountains were settled, before the hills was I brought forth: While as yet he had not made the earth; nor the fields, nor the highest part of the dust of the world. When he prepared the heavens, I was there: when he set a compass upon the face of the depth: When he established the clouds above: when he strengthened the fountains of the deep: When he gave the sea his decree, that the waters should not pass his commandment: when he appointed the foundations of the earth: Then I was by him, as one brought up with him: and I was daily his delight, rejoicing always before him: Rejoicing in the habitable part of his earth;

and my delights were with were with the sons of men. Now therefore hearken unto me, O ye children: for blessed are they that keep my ways. Hear instruction, and be wise, and refuse it not. Blessed is the man that hearth me, watching daily at my gates, waiting at the posts of my doors. For whoso findeth me findeth life, and shall obtain favor of the Lord. But he that sinneth against me wrought his own soul: all they that hate me love death.

Proverbs 8:22–36

The works of wisdom are so multifaceted and astonishing! When I read this biographical account of wisdom, I realize the love that the father has for his children. Wisdom tells of her very notable and majestic credentials as one that was with the Lord from the beginning of time. How she along with the Lord found pleasure in man and how she has devoted herself to the well-being of God's children. Then firmly she warns us to listen to her because she knows the ways of God and can cause us to surpass and defeat every obstacle in our lives. Wisdom, the capacity enlarger, continues to instruct us to use good judgment and knowledge and not to reject her guidance if we want to be blessed. She makes it clear that she has been charged with bringing enlargement to every part of our lives if we would only obey her.

A New Look at Jabez

Several years ago, much of the body of Christ, read, sung, and made quotes pertaining to Jabez. We were very inspired by the scriptures about Jabez because they offered hope to us. Like Jabez, we too had great needs in our lives, and we yearned to know how we might be able to get God to bless us just as he had Jabez. Due to our hunger to be blessed by God, these two verses of scripture from the Bible that reference Jabez resounded around the world. It was as though our declaring of these scriptures alone would cause the same blessing of God to come upon us.

First Chronicles 4:9–10 says,

> And Jabez was more honourable than this brethren: and his mother called his name Jabez, saying, Because I bare him with sorrow. And Jabez called on the God of Israel, saying, Oh that thou wouldest bless me indeed, and enlarge my coast, and that thine hand might be with me, and that thou wouldest keep me from evil, that it may not grieve me! And God granted him that which he requested.

In all of our euphoria, maybe many of us never received answers or manifestations to our prayers because we never considered why God blessed, praised, and declared that Jabez was more honorable than his brothers.

Could Jabez have been more honorable than his brothers because his brothers were entangled with pagan worship and idolatry? Perhaps Jabez unselfishly had cared for his mother who had birthed him in mental anguish. Maybe God allowed a break through in Jabez's life because of a covenant that he had made with one of Jabez's descendants in years past. In studying, I surprisingly learned that Jabez was a descendant of Judah, who was one of the twelve sons of Jacob whose name was changed by God to Israel. Israel blessed and prophesied over Judah the coming of the Messiah. Through the loins of Judah, Jabez became a part of the ancestry of Jesus Christ (Matthew 1:3). Could many years later Jabez be receiving the results of a generational blessing that had been spoken over Judah by his father Israel upon his deathbed? (Genesis 49:8–12, 33)

I don't know what caused Jabez to be different from his brothers. What I do know is that Jabez humbled himself and cried out in reverence and desperation to the God of Israel and God heard him! As Jabez honors God by calling out to him, God in turn answers him and gives him the desires of his heart; thereby reciprocating his love and approval for Jabez.

I believe that the spirit of wisdom caused Jabez to realize that if he didn't call out to God and allow him to do something new in his life that he too would be overtaken by the generational curse of depression, deprivation, suffering and lack which had overtaken his mother. There is no doubt that the same generational curse was patiently awaiting the opportunity to completely seize Jabez and fulfill the curse that had been pronounced upon him at birth.

Jabez renounced the curse and took hold of the opportunity being afforded him. He immediately cries out to almighty God, the only true and living God, which defies the meaning of his birth name, "son of sorrow". Today Jabez is known as a young man whose prayer God heard and answered. He has shown us the power of calling on God and the importance of positioning your heart to receive honor and blessings. There is no doubt that when wisdom spoke and Jabez answered the call, that there was a sudden change and shifting that resulted in the reversal of the course of Jabez's life. This new encounter with wisdom caused Jabez to immediately advance into new levels of victory in every area of his life.

Jabez now steps back into his rightful place of spiritual and natural prosperity all because he answered Wisdom's call and cried out to the Lord God. Proverbs 9:10 says, "The fear of the Lord is the beginning of wisdom; and the knowledge of the holy is understanding." Honor, respect, and loyalty for God are the ways that we fear and reverence him. These are characteristics that will cause one to walk before God in truth, with all of their heart and soul. These qualities will arrest the heart of God and cause him to add another fifteen years to your life as he did for Hezekiah, make the sun and moon stand still as he did for Joshua while he defeated his enemy, remember his covenant as he did with David or give you the desire of your heart as he did for Jabez. True love and reverence for the Lord are expressions and manifestations, which can only be communicated when wisdom abides. Wisdom allows us to discern what God holds in high esteem, what he considers sacred or set apart and then helps us to line up with God's will; that is why I call Wisdom "the capacity enlarger".

Heed Wisdom's Call

Doth not wisdom cry? And understanding put forth her voice? She standeth in the top of high places, by the way in the places of the paths. She crieth at the gates, at the entry of the city, at the coming in at the doors. Unto you, O men, I call; and my voice is to the sons of man. O ye simple, understand wisdom: and; ye fools, be ye of an understanding heart. Hear; for I speak of excellent things; and the opening of my lips shall be right things. For my mouth shall speak truth; and wickedness is an abomination to my lips. Proverbs 8:1–7

Jabez heard the voice of wisdom calling and he received her and reaped the benefits. Today she continues to make the universal, clarion call to us from every highway and hedge encouraging us to receive her. It is her desire to tell us great and mighty things. She wants to enlarge our capacity. It is her passion to see us increased, expanded, and stretched in every area of our lives spiritually, naturally, financially, mentally, and relationally. Wisdom endeavors to make us more than conquerors as we align our mind, soul, body, and spirit with the will of the Father. Whatever we set our hearts and minds to do for the kingdom of heaven and for ourselves will be accomplished without a struggle.

For Wisdom Is Better Than Rubies

For many of us money has been the number one reason for our struggle. That is probably because we have not had enough money to accomplish what we have deemed important. Everyone knows that we need money to live in this world; however, wisdom says,

> Receive my instruction, and not silver, and knowledge rather than choice gold. For wisdom is better than rubies; and all the things that may be desired are not to be compared to it. I wisdom dwell with prudence, and find out knowledge of witty inventions... I love them that love me; and those that seek me early shall find me. Riches and honour are with me; yea, durable, riches and righteousness. My fruit is better than gold, yea; than fine gold; and my revenue than choice silver. I lead in the way of righteousness, in the midst of the paths of judgment: That I may cause those that love me to inherit substance; and I will fill their treasure.
>
> Proverbs 8:10–21

Wisdom, *the capacity enlarger,* gives us insight on how to live without lack. She instructs us to take the sensible course and to stop seeking after money and start pursuing her. She teaches that money is important, however, that it does not offer the long-lasting stability that she can give us. That is because she is the source or initiator of where all monies come from. Wisdom boldly speaks out and tells of her ability to give us new ideas, insights, and concepts that the world has never thought of. This is because she dwells with our Father God and understands how to prosper his people.

Well Are You Going to Ask?

The world has told us for years to go after the gold and acquire all of the money that you can get. While wisdom has been crying out for thousands of years that we are going the wrong way. We should follow her because our Father has given her specific instructions on how he can and wants to increase us. Knowing the will of God for increase in my life, I have made the simple but wise decision to follow after wisdom. Thereby, not just being a hearer of the Word of God but also being a doer of the Word of God. James 1:5 says, "If any man lack wisdom, let him ask of God, that giveth to all men liberally, and upbraideth not; and it shall be given him." God has given us instruction to ask for wisdom if we don't have it, so that we might be a wise people that call on the name of the Lord. God knew that wisdom would remove mediocrity and give us greatness. Wisdom, *the capacity enlarger,* causes greatness because it challenges us to function at our maximum level. When we function at our maximum level, our achievements and performances are a cut above our counterparts, and we become more distinguished because we are abiding in the wisdom of God. Wisdom will cause the struggle to be over because the kingdom of heaven has come. What are you waiting for? *Ask for wisdom!*

Like Jabez, you too will have wisdom activated and operational in your life and thereby cause God to respond favorably to your prayers, inevitably seeing the miraculous as it happen for you!

Chapter 10

GREAT DROPS
OF BLOOD

*The Importance of Living
a Disciplined Life*

You and I will probably never realize the agony
and suffering that Jesus endured in the Garden of
Gethsemane as he prayed and made his final prep-
arations before going to the cross. Many of us saw
the movie *The Passion of the Christ* by Mel Gibson.
I believe this movie to be the best depiction of the
suffering and discipline of Christ. It was so real
that many of us could not stand to watch the pain,
suffering, and agony that Jesus submitted himself
to on our behalf . We covered our faces with our
hands, turned our heads away, and sobbed uncon-
trollably. I wonder how many of us thought about

the word discipline one time as we watched Jesus endure this excruciating pain, pain that he did not deserve. As God's children, I don't believe that many of us know what true discipline is. The discipline that God requires of us causes us to give up our will for his will, which means that we can no longer do things the way we want to. Instead we must totally submit to and obey God wholeheartedly in every area of our lives. In order for us to do this, we will have to mortify or put to death our flesh, and this can only be done by submitting to the Spirit of God. God's Spirit is the only power that is capable of giving us the ability to discipline our body (flesh) and cause it to line up with the Word of God.

We know that Jesus is the Son of God; he was born of a woman and came to earth to redeem us back to the Father. We also know that as the Son of God, Jesus never used his godly powers to escape the suffering and agony that he was asked to submit to by his Father. The scriptures say,

> Forasmuch then as the children are partakers of flesh and blood, he also himself likewise took part of the same; that through death he might destroy him that had the power of death, that is the devil ... For verily he took not on him the nature of angels; but he took on him the seed of Abraham. Wherefore in all things it behoved him to be made like unto his brethren, that he might be a merciful and faithful high priest in things pertaining to God, to make reconciliation for the sins of the people. For in that he himself hath suffered being tempted, he is able to succour them that are tempted.
>
> Hebrews 2:14–18

When I read this scripture, it lets me know without a doubt that Jesus was flesh and blood just like you and I. The only difference I see between Christ and many of us today is that Christ wanted to please his Father. Therefore, he disciplined and aligned himself with the will of the Father so that he would do as the Father requested of him. Yes, even to his death on the cross.

The Call to Discipline

Disciplining oneself is no small thing in the eyes of God, especially when we are talking about the kingdom. Discipline and obedience go together in our lives, and you will never find one without the other. When one disciplines oneself, they usually submit to training that will produce specific characteristics or patterns of behavior. While discipline is a systematic method used to obtain obedience and is based upon submission to rules and authority, many times discipline comes through experiences that are not so pleasing or gratifying to our flesh, such as fasting. From my personal experience, I know that self-discipline requires a heart that loves the Father and that is sold out to him. When we are in love with Father God, our desire will always be to exhibit immediate obedience no matter how difficult it may be.

Paul the Apostle said,

And every man that striveth for the mastery is temperate in all things. Now they do it to obtain a corruptible crown; but we an incorruptible. I therefore so run, not as uncertainly; so fight I, not as one that beateth the air: But I keep under my body, and bring it into subjection: lest that by any means, when I have preached to others, I myself should be a castaway.

1 Corinthians 9:25–26

Paul makes the statement that if one will choose to rule or discipline their flesh, they must have balance, stability, and fortitude, even when their flesh is screaming, kicking, and crying to do its own will and telling you that it cannot go any further. No matter how much our flesh tries to rebel against us, we must do as Paul did and keep it under subjection. If you choose not to, one day you will realize that your flesh has become king and is now ruling you. I believe that to find oneself without discipline is to find oneself out of the will of God.

There is no doubt that Jesus was disciplined in every area of his life and that he placed his Father's will above his very own.

Luke 22:39–44 says,

And he came out, and went, as he was wont, to the mount of Olives; and his disciples also followed him. And when he was at the place, he said unto them, Pray that ye enter not in to temptation. And he was withdrawn from them about a stone's cast, and kneeled down, and prayed, Saying if thou be willing, remove this cup from me: nevertheless not my will but thine, be done. And there appeared and angel unto him from heaven, strengthening him. And being in agony he prayed more earnestly: and his sweat was as it were great drops of blood falling down to the ground.

Jesus in the Garden of Gethsemane had already begun to experience the agony of the sins of the world, which he had to carry to the cross in obedience to his Father's will. Without walking in discipline, the power of the Holy Spirit, and the will of God, neither Jesus nor anyone else would have been capable of fulfilling such an enormous call. Thanks be to God that Jesus understood the importance of his purpose on earth and that he (Jesus) was willing to fulfill it. Jesus knew that God's plan would not be an easy one but that it was a necessary one. As followers of Christ, we must commit to becoming more dedicated and disciplined. We must lay down every excuse for not doing what we have been asked by God to do and allow the power of the Holy Spirit to help us just as he did Jesus, as he obediently went to Calvary.

If Jesus is our example, and that he is, we also must be willing to obediently follow our Father even to the cross. As you read these scriptures, I would ask you to see Jesus not as the suffering Savior but as the obedient son that gave his life in obedience to his Father. Perhaps this will help you as you decide to walk in obedience to the Father.

As many were astonied at thee; his visage was so marred more than any man, and his form more than the sons of men: So shall he sprinkle many nations; the kings shall shut their mouths at him: for that which had not been told them shall they see; and that which they had not heard shall they consider. Who hath believed our report? And to whom is the arm of the Lord revealed? For he shall grow up before him as a tender plant, and as a root out of a dry ground: he hath no form nor comeliness; and when we shall see him, there is no beauty that we should desire him. He is despised and rejected of men; a man of sorrows and acquainted with grief: and we hid as it were our faces from him; he was despised, and we esteemed him not. Surely he hath borne our griefs, and carried our sorrows: yet we did esteem him stricken, smitten of God and afflicted. But he was wounded for our transgressions, he was bruised for our iniquities: the chastisement of our peace was upon him; and with his stripes we are healed. All we like sheep have gone astray; we have turned everyone to his own way: and the Lord hath laid on him the iniquity of us all. He was oppressed, and he was afflicted yet he opened not his mouth: he is brought as a lamb to the slaughter, and as a sheep before her shearers is dumb, so he openeth not his mouth. He was taken from prison and from judgment: and who shall declare his generation? For he was cut off out of the land of the living: for the transgression of my people was he stricken. And he made his grave with the wicked, and with the rich in his death; because he had done no violence, neither was any deceit in his mouth. Yet it pleased the Lord to bruise him; he hath put him to grief: when thou shalt make his soul an offering for sin, he shall see his seed he shall prolong his days, and the pleasure of the Lord shall prosper in his hand. He shall see of the travail of his soul, and shall be satisfied: by his knowledge shall my righteous servant justify many; for he shall bear their iniquities. Therefore will I divide him a portion with the great, and he shall divide the spoil with the strong; because he hath poured out his soul unto death: and he was numbered with the transgressors; and he bare the sins of many, and made intercession for the transgressors.

Isaiah 52:14–53:12

After reading these scriptures and looking back on the movie *The Passion of the Christ,* we can clearly see how important it was for Jesus to be disciplined as he suffered at Calvary. For without his sacrifice, there would have not been redemption for us, and we would have remained slaves of Satan.

Thankfully God has not asked us to die on a cross, but he is asking that we pick up our cross and follow him by submitting our all to him through discipline and obedience.

Jesus has called us to be his disciples. As a disciple, one follows the teachings of his master. The words *discipline* and *disciple* both have the same root word, *discere,* which means to learn. To learn is to gain knowledge, comprehension, or mastery of through experience or study. As Christ's disciples we must learn to become disciplined and follow our leader example. We have no choice; it is required of every disciple. Just as Jesus learned obedience by the things that he suffered; we too must learn to carry out the request and commands of our Father. Even if it means that we must endure pain, injury, or punishment for the cause of Christ in the new millennium.

Our God is a God of excellence. Excellence in the things of God or anything else will always require discipline, and that will always cost us something, whether it is our money, time, or physical labor. Where there is no sacrifice there will be no glory! Where there is no cross; there will be no crown! So what's our excuse? We have none; they were all nailed to the cross on Calvary.

> ... Looking to Jesus the authority and finisher of our faith; who for the joy that was set before him endured the cross, despising the same, and is set down at the right hand of the throne of God. For consider him that endured such contradiction of sinners against himself, lest ye be wearied and faint in your minds. Ye have not yet resisted unto blood, striving against sin.
>
> Hebrews 12:2–4

Chapter 11

THE GOSPEL OF SALVATION

The Good News

For God so loved the world, that he gave his only begotten Son, that whosoever believeth in him should not perish, but have everlasting life. For God sent not his Son into the world to condemn the world; but that the world through him might saved.

John 3:16–17

This is one of the first scriptures that I ever learned and one that gives me great confidence of God's love for me. Jesus' words let me know that my salvation is secure in him if I would only believe. Accepting Jesus as my personal savior has been the best thing that has ever happened to me, and I believe this to be the testimony of many others as well. As I look back over my life as a believer in Jesus Christ, man's tradition and religion has kept me focused primarily on the gospel of salvation. Not until the last ten years or so, have I heard anyone talk about the kingdom of God with such revelation, understanding, and intensity. Could it be that we never had a true understanding of the purpose of the gospel of salvation?

Revelation, the Eye Opener

For the most part, salvation in terms of redemption has been Christian's focal point. Rightly so since God did send his only begotten Son to die on the cross for us, which is not a small matter. Never would I devalue Christ's suffering and sacrifice for our sins. To do so would be to spit in the face of Christ. Only his blood could have provided the atonement that we needed to be made the righteousness of God. However, Jesus' death and resurrection was not only for payment of our sins, it was also to get us back into right relationship with the Father. God's plan from the beginning was that his son's death would also allow us to rule and reign again just as we had before Adam and Eve's disobedience in the garden of Eden. Salvation in the truest sense is that there should be nothing missing or nothing broken in any area of our lives. Simply put, there should be no lack anywhere and at anytime in our lives. Therefore, salvation is whatever we need: deliverance, safety, and victory, as well as spiritual and physical prosperity.

Instead of us seeing what God saw for us through the death and resurrection of his Son, many have only seen salvation as a means to escape hell's fire and to have eternal life. For a long time, we haven't seen ourselves fulfilling all that God predestined for us from the foundation of the world, which includes kingdom living. As we grew up in Christendom, the good news of forgiveness from our sins—or should I say the gospel of reconciliation—was all that we were taught and knew. Therefore, this teaching caused many of us to only be concerned about staying "saved" so that we could receive our mansion over in glory one day. We didn't understand that we could have eternal life and our mansions now.

I believe that salvation is like a first fruit of faith. Accepting Christ as our Savior and Lord is just the beginning. It is the door that we open which allows us to walk into greatness as believers. Jesus said, "Behold, I stand at the door, and knock: if any man hear my voice, and open the door, I will come into him, and will sup with him, and he with me" (Revelation 3:20). It is this step of faith that gives the believer unlimited opportunities as we walk in all that the kingdom of God afford us. Jesus invites us to greatness as we have fellowship with him and become one with him just as he was one with his Father. When we walk in unity, we will fulfill the will of the Father here on the earth. If we are unable, however, to trust Father God with our life—the one which gave us our very life—how can he trust us with the kingdom? Therefore, faith to believe that God is able to save us is the first fruit of faith.

Salvation and the gospel of the kingdom go hand in hand. Both play a very vital part in the plans that God has for us. When Nicodemus came to Jesus by night because he wanted to know the truth regarding salvation, "Jesus answered and said unto him, Verily, verily, I say unto thee, Except a man be born again, he cannot see the kingdom of God" (St. John 3:3). Then Jesus went on to tell Nicodemus, "Verily, verily, I say unto thee, Except a man be born of water and of the Spirit, he cannot enter into the kingdom of God. That which is born of the flesh is flesh; and that which is born of the Spirit is spirit. Marvel not that I said unto thee, Ye must be born again" (St. John 3:5–7).

How many times have we read and quoted this scripture regarding salvation yet overlooked the vast importance of the kingdom of God being apart of the will of God for his children? I don't believe that Jesus was just talking about the kingdom of God when we get to heaven. Jesus was letting Nicodemus know that even though we are fleshly beings when we are joined to him we become spiritual beings in a fleshly body. This changes our citizenship from earth to heaven and we are not to operate by the world's standards anymore. We are now to operate by God's standards. We cannot focus solely on salvation because the Father intended for us to have so much more. Salvation allows us to go to the next level. It provides the basic fundamentals of trust in the Father and his Son, thereby giving us a solid foundation that we are able to build upon. We are then able to operate as one with the Father and his son.

As Jesus prepared to leave earth, he authorized and gave the disciples the power to carry out kingdom business here on the earth. Jesus said,

> Go ye into all the world, and preach the gospel to every creature. He that believeth and is baptized shall be saved; but he that believeth not shall be damned. And these signs shall follow them that believe; In my name shall they cast out devils; they shall speak with new tongues; They shall take up serpents; and if they drink any deadly thing, it shall not hurt them; they shall lay hands on the sick, and they shall recover. So then after the Lord had spoken unto them, he was received up into heaven and sat on the right hand of God. And they went forth, and preached everywhere, the Lord working with them, and confirming the word with signs following. Amen.
>
> Mark 16:15–20

Just as these believers were commissioned, we have been commissioned as well to preach the gospel. This will show that the manifestations of the kingdom of heaven has come to earth and they can be seen through us the "believers"! We must teach and tell the truth and nothing but the truth. Of course, salvation is the will of God; however, salvation and the kingdom of heaven is the more complete will of God. As faith without works is dead, salvation without the kingdom of heaven is incomplete. Now that this has been revealed, and we now know better, we must do better.

Jesus said,

And that servant, which knew his lord's will, and prepared not himself, neither did according to his will, shall be beaten with many stripes. But he that knew not, and did commit things worthy of stripes, shall be beaten with few stripes. For unto whomsoever much is given, of him shall be much required: and to whom men have committed much, of him they will ask the more.

Luke 12:47–48

CONCLUSION

As we look back and see what God's desire and purpose has been for us from the foundation of the world; from the time that he placed the first man in the Garden of Eden and told him to subdue the land and have dominion; we see that we have been chosen to be a people of victory, destiny and dominion. As people of God we have been given authority to rule and reign right now on planet earth.

Therefore, I encourage you to take faith and take God at His word, for it is true. Stop the struggling; the self reliance, self rule, and dependence on yourself and others and start to trust God with all of your heart, mind, soul, and strength. For it is the will of God to bless you spiritually, physically, mentally, financially, and relationally. Proverbs 28:20 says, "A faithful man shall abound with blessings."

God's will and instructions for us to walk in dominion has never changed. What are we waiting for? Let's allow the power of the Holy Spirit to provide us with the wisdom and knowledge that we need to be an over comer in all areas of our lives and stop the struggling.

Who is he that condemneth? It is Christ that died, yea rather that is risen again, who is even at the right hand of God, who also maketh intercession for us. Who shall separate us from the love of Christ? Shall tribulation, or distress, or persecution, or famine, or nakedness, or peril, or sword? As it is written, for thy sake we are killed all the daylong; we are accounted as sheep for the slaughter. *Nay, in all these things we are more than conquerors through him that loved us. For I am persuaded, that neither death, nor life, nor angels, nor principalities, nor powers, nor things present, nor things to come, nor height, nor depth, nor any other creature, shall be able to separate us from the love of God, which is in Christ Jesus our Lord.*

Romans 8:34–39

As we endeavor to walk in obedience and trust in our Father; let us never forget the words of Jesus:

Therefore I say unto you, Take no thought for your life, what ye shall eat, or what ye shall drink; nor yet for your body, what ye shall put on. Is not the life more than meat, and the body than raiment? Behold the fowls of the air: for they sow not, neither do they reap, nor gather into barns; yet your heavenly Father feedeth them. Are ye not much better than they? Which of you by taking thought can add one cubit unto his stature? And why take ye thought for raiment? Consider the lilies of the field, how they grow; they toil not, neither do they spin: And yet I say unto you, that even Solomon in all his glory was not arrayed like one of these. Wherefore, if God so clothe the grass of the field, which today is, and tomorrow is cast into the oven, shall he not much more clothe you, O ye of little faith? Therefore take no thoughts, saying, what shall we eat? Or, what shall we drink? Or, wherewithal shall we be clothed? (For after all these things do the Gentiles seek:) for your heavenly Father knoweth that ye have need of all these things. *But seek ye first the kingdom of God, and his righteousness and all of these things shall be added unto you.* Take therefore no thought for the morrow: for the morrow shall take thought for the things of itself. Sufficient unto the day is the evil thereof.

Matthew 6:25–34

BIBLIOGRAPHY

Edwell, Walter A., and Baker Book House, eds. "Kingdom of God." *Baker Theological Dictionary of the Bible.* 2000. 95 & 451.

Message, The. Colorado Springs, CO: NavPress, 1993.

Thompson Chain Reference Study Bible KJV. 5th ed. London: B.B. Kirkbride Bible Company Inc., 2004.

ENDNOTES

I   The heart of Jesus' teachings centers around the theme of the kingdom of God. This expression is found in sixty-one separate sayings in the Synoptic Gospels. (Designating the first three Gospels of the New Testament, which correspond closely.) Counting parallels (Readily recognized similarities) to these passages, the expression occurs over eighty-five times.

It was once popular in certain circles to argue that the expressions "kingdom of God" and "kingdom of heaven" referred to two different realities. It is now clear, however, that they are synonyms. This is evident for several reasons. For one, the two expressions are used in the same sayings of Jesus, but Matthew uses "kingdom of heaven" Mark or Luke or both use "kingdom of God." Second, Matthew himself uses these two expressions interchangeably in (Matthew 19:23–24).

Baker Theological Dictionary of the Bible

2 Scriptures to support that the kingdom of heaven has come:

" … for your heavenly Father knoweth that ye have need of all these things. *But seek ye first the kingdom of God and his righteousness;* and all of these things shall be added to you. Take no thought for the morrow: for the morrow shall take thought for the things of itself. Sufficient unto the day is the evil thereof." (Matthew 6:31–34)

"Now after that John was put in prison, Jesus came into Galilee, *preaching the gospel of the kingdom of God.*" And saying, "*The time is ful-filled, and the kingdom of God is at hand:* repent ye, and believe the gospel." (Mark 1:14)

"I must preach the *kingdom of God* to other cit-ies also: for therefore am I sent." (Luke 4:43)

"Then he called his twelve disciples together, and gave them power and authority over all devils, and to cure diseases. And he sent them *to preach the kingdom of God,* and to heal the sick." (Luke 9:2)

"The law and the prophets were until John: since that time the *kingdom of God is preached,* and every man presseth into it." (Luke 16:16)

"Until the day in which he was taken up, after that he through the Holy Ghost had given commandments unto the apostles whom he had chosen: To whom also he shewed himself alive after his passion by many infallible proofs, being seen of them forty days, and *speaking of the things pertaining to the kingdom of God:* and, being assembled together with them, commanded them that they should depart from Jerusalem, but wait for the promise of the father, which, saith he, ye have heard of me." (Acts 1:2–4)

"And when he was demanded of the Pharisees, when the kingdom of God should come, he answered them and said, The kingdom of God cometh not with observation: Neither shall they say, Lo here! or, lo there! for, behold the kingdom of God is within you." (Luke 17:20–21)

⊖|LIVE

listen|imagine|view|experience

AUDIO BOOK DOWNLOAD INCLUDED WITH THIS BOOK!

In your hands you hold a complete digital entertainment package. Besides purchasing the paper version of this book, this book includes a free download of the audio version of this book. Simply use the code listed below when visiting our website. Once downloaded to your computer, you can listen to the book through your computer's speakers, burn it to an audio CD or save the file to your portable music device (such as Apple's popular iPod) and listen on the go!

How to get your free audio book digital download:

1. Visit www.tatepublishing.com and click on the e|LIVE logo on the home page.
2. Enter the following coupon code:
   dc4e-dc92-5439-d423-6ea7-1ba9-9d59-daa7
3. Download the audio book from your e|LIVE digital locker and begin enjoying your new digital entertainment package today!